Portraits of Promise

Portraits of Promise

Voices of Successful Immigrant Students

Michael Sadowski

HARVARD EDUCATION PRESS
CAMBRIDGE, MASSACHUSETTS

Youth Development
and Education Series

Copyright © 2013 by the President and Fellows of Harvard College

Library of Congress Control Number 2012951227
Paperback ISBN 978-1-61250-516-9
Library Edition ISBN 978-1-61250-517-6

Published by Harvard Education Press,
an imprint of the Harvard Education Publishing Group

Harvard Education Press
8 Story Street
Cambridge, MA 02138

Cover Design: Sarah Henderson

Cover Photos: ©iStockphoto.com/Jbryson (girl top left)/hartcreations (boy
bottom left)/alejandrophotography (girl top right)/kupicoo (boy bottom right)

The typefaces used in this book are Berkeley Old Style, ITC Legacy Sans,
and Ruzicka.

CONTENTS

PART ONE

Meeting on the Coasts

PART TWO

The Portraits

PART THREE

Living Up to the Promise

FOREWORD

REMARKABLY DIVERSE IMMIGRANT-ORIGIN youth are the fastest growing sector of our nation's student population today. Some are the children of highly educated professional parents who have received initial schooling in exemplary educational systems, while others arrive with interrupted schooling from educational systems that are in shambles. Some newcomers arrive to welcoming school contexts while others encounter schools ill-prepared to serve them. While some immigrant students demonstrate worrisome school-related problems and high dropout rates, others outperform their native-born peers.[1] Though there is a growing body of research literature on the obstacles that low-achieving students in particular encounter, often this work does little to shed light on either the lived experiences of these students or practical steps that educators can take. In *Portraits of Promise*, Michael Sadowski turns to newcomer adolescent students who are successfully navigating their educational voyage and asks them to share their trials, tribulations, insights, and wisdom.

Sensibly, Sadowski turns to adolescents as his informants. Urban Institute researchers Ruiz-de-Velasco, Fix, and Clewell have found that students arriving after age thirteen are particularly at risk of being "overlooked and underserved" as students.[2] Although approximately half of immigrant-origin students who enter our public school system arrive at secondary school age, many of the educational interventions for newcomers are designed for the primary grades. Students arriving during middle school or high school encounter particular challenges as they not only need to play catch-up academically but also need to acquire academic English language proficiency while accruing all the credits required to graduate and pass high-stakes tests in a time frame comparable to their native-born peers. They are also facing all the usual developmental challenges of adolescents when finding their place in the world, and articulating a clear identity reigns as a central preoccupation. This age group, however, is exceptionally articulate and insightful and can, when interviewed by an empathic and interested listener, clearly state what they (and their less successful peers) need in order to do well.

In these beautifully rendered portraits, Michael Sadowski captures the perspectives and voices of immigrant newcomer adolescents. Every portrait convincingly captures the unique experience of each adolescent, yet as someone who has been a therapist, high school guidance counselor, elementary, middle, and high school psychologist, university researcher, and graduate mentor of immigrant-origin students for over two dozen years, I can vouch that each of the eight portraits also encapsulates the experiences of hundreds more like them. These are not exceptional kids—I have met many versions of other students like them over the years. If readers carefully listen to these eloquent young people's points of view—gently but expertly elicited by Sadowski's empathic interviewing—they will feel like they know each child and will have the opportunity to "walk in her shoes." Sadowski also provides immensely practical and wise advice that will empower *both* first-year teachers as well as highly experienced teachers and administrators to understand and work with the new student populations encountered in our rapidly changing schools across the country.

Without giving away the punch lines of this highly readable and engaging book, here are some of the unforgettable take-home messages that bear highlighting. For newcomer students (be they immigrants or not), the first weeks and months in a new school are always daunting and disorienting. This is compounded all the more for immigrant students who contend with new languages, new cultural expectations, and new schooling practices. All too often either teachers (*see Diana*) or peers (*see Ibrahim*) serve as tormentors to newcomers instead of mentors in the early transition. (To this day, I will never forget, as a newcomer student, the sting of my peers' roar of laughter after the history teacher blurted out, "Oh, that sounds just like a toilet flushing!" following her asking me to say my rather odd maiden name after stumbling across it for the first time on the roster.) Teachers and administrators can make all the difference in making the transition as minimally traumatic as possible. By providing peer liaisons, allowing use of both English and native languages to establish basic understanding, providing adult mentors, and having a zero tolerance for tormenting, that initial period, while never easy, can serve as a welcoming bridge into the new society.

Most immigrant students arrive to their new schools with remarkable optimism and hope about the future. They do not take their educations for granted, and they recognize that schooling is the key to a better tomorrow. This is something to be cultivated first by recognizing strengths and resiliencies (rather than focusing on deficiencies and obstacles), by maintaining high expectations while remaining *patient* (as both the young informants and Sadowski poignantly remind us) with the time it takes to make the journey to educational success.

Relationships, at many levels, make *all the difference* in fostering the academic engagement and resilience unveiled in this powerful book. Students are often highly motivated by the sacrifices made by their parents on their behalf—though they may be the first to make that journey on to college, they do it not just for themselves but for their parents (*see Ricky*) and for their communities; this is a powerful motivator all too often forgotten by educators that can and should be harnessed. Students can (and often do) support one another, and this can be all the more potent if fostered astutely through school and afterschool activities. Of course, teachers and other adults in schools are often behind the success of the students who flourish most—being that "special teacher" (*see Eduardo*) can, and often does, make all the difference in students' lives. Relationships at all these levels serve to help immigrant students through difficult transitions. They help in making sense of new cultural and linguistic rules of engagement. Relationships can provide information about how to interview for a job or how to apply to college or about how to negotiate other relationships. Relationships with teachers can get students excited about an academic subject and keep students engaged in doing the work when the distractions of life occur. And relationships can help students maintain confidence in themselves if they flounder. Of course, these crucial relationships (with peers, with family, with teachers) are necessary for most students. They may be even more essential for newcomers, who need that extra beacon of light in a foggy new world.

Immerse yourself into these young people's lives; Michael Sadowski is an expert tour guide. You will know these eight adolescents as if you had met them yourself, and in turn you will feel both inspired and empowered to engage with your own newcomer students.

Carola Suárez-Orozco
Professor of Psychological Studies in Education
University of California, Los Angeles

INTRODUCTION

Hearing the Voices of Success

THREE PEDIATRICIANS, an architect, a biochemist, a computer scientist, and nineteen college graduates are among the people readers may encounter in *Portraits of Promise*. To be more precise, these are some of the future selves to which the successful middle and high school students I interviewed for the book aspire. Although the ambitions of teenagers obviously change as they finish high school, enter college, and develop new interests, the contributions these high-achieving young people could make to our society in the next decade or so defy prediction. The purpose of this book is to understand better what factors contribute to the success of high-achieving immigrant middle and high school students so that we might nurture it more effectively and help them, as well as their peers, make their aspirations a reality.

Despite the assets that many young people bring from their homes and cultures of origin, immigrant students who excel academically do so against considerable odds. Students from immigrant families—roughly one in four students currently living in the United States—are vastly more likely than their peers to live in poverty, to speak a language other than English at home, to attend under-resourced and ethnically segregated schools, and to experience other factors that have been associated with academic risk in U.S. schooling contexts.[1] If they live in urban

1

settings, immigrant youth are more likely than other youth to live in neighborhoods where street crime is an ever-present threat.[2] For young people who are newcomers to the U.S. themselves, these risks can be exacerbated by others associated with immigration, which in some cases include being refugees from war or other dire conditions in their countries of origin; long-term separation from one or both parents; the daily stress their families' experience if they are undocumented; and the disequilibrium that can arise from learning what it means to be a student in a new schooling context, one that may be quite different from the one they were accustomed to in their country of origin—if they have any history of consistent formal education at all.[3] Finally, children from immigrant families are often subject to what researcher Angela Valenzuela has called "subtractive schooling," whereby educational institutions are designed to, in effect, "subtract" their original languages and cultures based on the mistaken belief that they are deficits standing in the way of their progress instead of assets that can be capitalized on along with learning English and acculturation to being American.[4]

These challenges and others contribute to academic failure and school dropout for far too many immigrant children as they reach middle and high school age.[5] Other immigrant adolescents, such as the ones interviewed for this book, however, thrive in U.S. school settings or, at the very least, succeed at exhibiting one or more behaviors that researchers have associated not only with being a successful student but with following a positive life trajectory after adolescence. Although most of the students interviewed for this project have high grade-point averages, students are considered successful for the purposes of this book if they do several of the following:

- engage with the culture of school in positive ways
- form strong bonds with teachers and know when, where, and how to ask for help
- develop their skills both in English and in academic subjects

- avoid negative peer pressure and violence and form positive peer networks that support, rather than hinder, their academic success
- manage the sometimes competing expectations of family and school
- negotiate the high-stakes terrain of standardized tests effectively
- draw upon their languages and cultures of origin as assets and complements to the learning of English (and to learning *in* English), using both cultures in ways that are "additive" rather than "subtractive"[6]
- learn how to apply to college—and be admitted—even if they are the first in their families to do so[7]

While none of these behaviors in and of themselves guarantees long-term academic, vocational, or personal success, all can have direct or indirect effects on an immigrant adolescent's overall level of achievement, school engagement, and future life chances.[8] Indeed, these are behaviors that can be viewed as key elements of success for all middle and high school students.[9] These are also behaviors that can be fostered by educators who have the knowledge, skills, and courage to create and maintain the kinds of learning environments that are most conducive to immigrant students' success.

ABOUT THIS BOOK: CONTEXT AND APPROACH

Important research has been published over the last several decades from sociology and other fields about the most recent waves of immigrants to the United States and the challenges they encounter as they attempt to forge new lives here. In addition to the poverty, unemployment or underemployment, and related economic problems that affect many, though certainly not all, immigrant families (especially if they arrive with limited resources), newcomers to the U.S. are subject to other challenges that are perhaps less measurable but no less damaging than socioeconomic ones. These include racist and anti-immigrant attitudes, fears that they are taking jobs away from Americans, and antipathy toward the languages they bring with them, based on the assumption that the United States should be a strictly English-speaking nation.[10] In recent years, these sorts of societal attitudes have been manifest in measures in certain states (most notably Arizona) aimed at restricting immigration, requiring immigrants to carry documentation at all times, deporting undocumented immigrants, and detaining any individuals suspected to be illegal immigrants.

Anti-immigrant attitudes and the policy decisions motivated by them work their way into the consciousness of immigrant youth in various ways, and other research has focused specifically on the experiences of children either from immigrant families or those who are immigrants themselves. Much of this work has found that immigrant students, predictably, often begin their U.S. schooling experiences in a state of disorientation if their language of origin is not English, but that their school trajectories can then take widely divergent paths based on a host of factors. In their 2008 book *Learning a New Land*, researchers Carola Suárez-Orozco, Marcelo Suárez-Orozco, and Irina Todorova cited data from the extensive Longitudinal Immigrant Student Adaptation (LISA) study, which included more than three hundred immigrant students over five years, and noted that about two-thirds of the students in their sample showed a decline in academic performance over the five-year research period. About a third of their sample, however, either showed improvement in their academic performance or maintained high grade-point averages over the years of the study.[11] Examining a host of factors, Suárez-Orozco and her colleagues concluded that an interconnected web of engagement plays a significant role in the academic success of immigrant students. In addition to English proficiency and factors associated with the family, they noted that *behavioral engagement*—positive and consistent performance of the tasks required in "doing school" such as attendance, note-taking, listening and participating, and homework completion—plays an especially important role in the academic achievement of immigrant students. Moreover, two other types of engagement, *relational engagement*—"the extent to which students feel connected to their teachers, peers, and others in their schools"—and *cognitive engagement*—"the degree to which the students are engrossed and intellectually engaged in what they are learning"— strongly influence behavioral engagement and, thus, academic achievement.[12] Simply put, positive engagement in one of these areas is likely to be associated with positive engagement in another, thus increasing the likelihood that an immigrant student will have a high level of academic performance.

The idea for *Portraits of Promise* began with this nexus of engagement in mind and some questions related to it, in particular:

- What do immigrant student achievers themselves believe helps them to be successful in school?
- Although immigrant students obviously do not think of things in these terms, if these types of engagement do in fact work together to support achievement, what does this interaction look like in their day-to-day lives?
- What factors encourage them to engage with (or disengage from) teachers, peers, curriculum, and other aspects of their school lives?
- Finally, how do family-related factors and other factors outside of school motivate successful students to achieve?

Because I was most interested in learning what immigrant students thought about these issues (and not what *I* thought they thought), I decided to address these questions using a method that represents the merger of two approaches: qualitative research and education journalism. Working as a qualitative researcher, I conducted both focus groups and extensive one-on-one interviews with participants, many of which lasted an hour or longer. I focused largely on questions of identity and voice that have been central to my research and teaching for the last decade and are prominent in my edited book *Adolescents at School: Perspectives on Youth, Identity, and Education*.[13] Beyond what teachers or researchers might say about them, what do adolescents say about themselves? How are their self-perceptions influenced by the people and social forces around them? What relationships are important to them, and what difference do they make? How do they envision themselves in the future? Drawing on my journalistic background as an editor of the *Harvard Education Letter* and other publications, I then stepped back from extensive analysis of the interviews and allowed the expertise in *Portraits of Promise* to lie not with me, the writer, but with the *real* experts. The emphasis in this book is thus on the voices of these immigrant students, what *they say* matters to them on a daily basis and helps spur them on to success.

The first step toward finding out what successful immigrant students thought about these issues was to locate some who were doing well despite considerable challenges and were willing to talk about why. Toward this end, I identified two schools on opposite coasts of the United States with distinctly different immigrant populations for my interviews. While this relatively small group of students obviously cannot represent the attitudes and opinions of all successful immigrant students, especially since school, family, and community contexts play such important roles in their success, the consistencies in some of their answers—as well as the contrasts—offer some valuable insights.

ABOUT THE SCHOOLS

New York Global High School (NYGHS) is part of the New York City Department of Education and serves a population of students who have been in the United States for three years or fewer upon their enrollment.[14] This small public high school, serving a population of approximately 380 students in grades 9–12, is located in one of the poorest neighborhoods in New York City. Like many low-income urban neighborhoods, the area surrounding the school is in many ways a study in contrasts. It contains rich cultural diversity, vibrant small businesses, and a lovingly maintained community garden. Within the school, there is a palpable sense of community as students from Central and South

America, the Caribbean, Africa, Asia, and other parts of the world come together to learn. At the same time, waves of crime in the neighborhood have at times led school officials to direct students to walk only on certain blocks to and from school, and several participants in the *Portraits of Promise* interviews describe situations in which they felt targeted as immigrants and unsafe on the surrounding streets.

As a New York City public school, students attending NYGHS are required to take the state Regents exams in order to graduate, a daunting task for English-language learners, although they may request translations of certain parts of the tests into the languages of origin most commonly spoken in New York. The school places a heavy emphasis on preparation for these tests as well as on college attendance. In their senior year, all students are assigned an advisor to coordinate their college recommendations, and college preparatory activities are woven into an advisory class and several afterschool programs. There are at least fifteen languages of origin spoken at the school. Seating in most classrooms is arranged in work tables of five or six students each, sometimes to encourage same-language translation (particularly in the earlier grades) and at other times to encourage students from different cultures and languages of origin to work together.

Clarkson Community School (CCS) serves a mixed population of immigrant and U.S.-born students in an inland region of California, with students born outside the U.S. representing about 15 percent of the population. A large percentage of the students attending Clarkson have family members working in the area's agricultural industry (or, as many of the students describe it, "in the fields"), and a large proportion of students at the school are either first- or second-generation Mexican American. Most of the immigrant students at CCS would be considered, according to some definitions, members of the "1.5 generation": those who immigrated to the U.S. at a young age but have experienced the majority of their childhood and adolescence in the United States.[15] While in some ways their stories thus represent facets of the immigrant youth experience that are very different from those of the students attending

NYGHS, their lives are also similar to those of more recent immigrants in several important respects. Most have parents who speak little or no English and therefore speak predominantly Spanish at home. Many continue to feel strong cultural and familial ties to Mexico, and some spoke in their one-on-one interviews about the difficulties they experienced reconciling their parents' Mexican values and their own emerging values as U.S. teenagers. Also, many explained that their families struggle financially and that they therefore have significant concerns about being able to pay for college.

CCS serves a population of approximately two hundred students in grades 6–12. It is housed in a newly built facility that takes full advantage of the area's warm climate in its physical structure. Students pass between classes outdoors beneath trees and abundant sunshine, and spaces are brighter and considerably more plentiful than one would typically find in a New York City public school. Since the home language of many students is Spanish, some school staff members and a few teachers speak Spanish fluently and are available to translate when parents come in to discuss students' work (and some students perform this translation themselves). To accommodate the long work schedules of many parents in the area, students are in school from 8 a.m. to 5 p.m., and, as a result, teachers assign little homework in favor of giving students time during the school day to complete tasks. CCS offers college-level classes to students in the higher grades, the credits from which are transferable to many colleges, and, like NYGHS, places a heavy emphasis on preparation for college in the form of counseling, assistance with applications, and connecting students with financial aid opportunities.

ABOUT THE INTERVIEWS

I began preparing for the interview process by conducting initial meetings with students at both schools. At NYGHS, these initial meetings took place in 11th and 12th grade classrooms, since students at these grade levels were the most likely to have sufficient proficiency and confidence to participate in the interviews in English. At CCS, recruitment involved the full grade range, and students in grades 6–11 opted to participate. In both cases, I encouraged students to think about the notion of success broadly, not merely in terms of high grades but also in terms of the measures of success discussed at the beginning of this introduction (e.g., having strong relationships with teachers, knowing how and when to ask for help, avoiding peer pressure and violence). Making clear that their participation or nonparticipation would in no way affect their standing at school, I invited interested students to take home child assent and parental consent forms, the latter of which were translated into four languages at NYGHS (Arabic, Bengali, French, and Spanish) and into Spanish at CCS. Students could thus self-nominate for the interviews and decide for themselves whether they were "successful students" (although a review of most students' transcripts corroborated their own assessments).

At both sites, I then formed focus groups from among students who indicated interest and provided the proper consent documentation, and focus groups met twice at each site for approximately one hour. The first group session at each site focused primarily on overall success factors, and I asked students directly about the factors they believed were most responsible for their achievement. The second set of sessions dealt more specifically with relationships and the people that students said they relied on to help them do well in school. An introduction to the students and a synthesis of some of these focus group conversations, organized thematically by the main topics students discussed, is included in the chapter that follows.

Students also were asked to indicate whether they were interested in participating in one-on-one interviews. There was considerable overlap in the focus group and individual interview sample, but at both sites there also were students who, because of scheduling or other issues, participated in one interview format but not the other. Overall, nineteen students participated in one or both focus groups at their school site (most students attended two meetings), and fourteen completed

in-depth individual interviews. Students and their parents or guard-
ians also agreed to allow me to review their school transcripts and, in
some cases, visit their classrooms and/or read samples of their written
work. The eight "portraits of promise" in this book capture in-depth
some of the student voices I heard throughout this process. I have cho-
sen these portraits specifically to highlight several themes that proved
important to the entire project, most notably the relationships that have
helped these students thrive. In order to preserve the students' voices
as much as possible in these profiles, I quote from our interviews heav-
ily and with minimal interpretation, except in the brief commentaries
that synthesize each portrait and set it in the context of larger issues
found in prior research with immigrant youth. In addition, I present
excerpts from the students' interviews without correcting minor lapses
in grammar or removing idiosyncrasies of adolescent speech (such as
frequent use of the word "like"). I believe these reminders of both their
youth and, in some cases, their relatively recent acquisition of English,
underscore the depth of their insight and highlight their promise rather
than detracting from it.

In a concluding section that follows the portraits, "Living Up to
the Promise," I synthesize (with an open invitation to readers' further
interpretation) what I believe are some of the most important implications of the insights students shared for classroom and school practice.
Finally, in an afterword I look beyond schools and explore briefly what
it might look like for the United States to become a "culture of promise,"
one that recognizes the tremendous assets these young people bring to
the country and how we might best nurture their potential.

Portraits of Promise was originally conceived as a book mainly for educators, since a central hypothesis underlying this project is that teaching, curriculum, and other factors directly associated with schooling
matter a great deal in determining whether immigrant students fail or
succeed. Yet the more I talked to young people who were succeeding
in school despite sometimes formidable and ongoing challenges, the

more I realized that teachers, administrators, school counselors, and other school staff played but one set of important roles in the lives of immigrant students. Other key actors in the success stories of these students included parents, siblings, other family members, peers, institutional mentors, and others, all of whom—when conditions are optimal—work in concerted ways to help these young people succeed. Thus, I hope the student voices in this book can be heard not only by professionals working in schools but also by the many other adults who care about immigrant youth and their futures—and by those who make the policies that deeply affect their lives. In addition, I encourage educators and other adults to share the student profiles in this book with young people, particularly youth from immigrant families. They may well have strong opinions about what their peers have to say and may even see some of their own experiences represented in these pages, perhaps for the first time. For all of us, there are always important lessons to be learned listening to young people, and the words of these immigrant students who succeed despite conditions that might predict failure may help us envision more effective schools not only for them but for all students.

PART ONE

Meeting on the Coasts

The New York and California Students

ALTHOUGH IN ONE SENSE I had met all the students interviewed in New York and California previously when I invited them and their classmates to participate in the project, I had little sense of what to expect when we gathered for the focus groups. How forthcoming would students be in answering my questions? How much would they be willing to engage with one another to delve into topics that arose and to express agreement or disagreement with their peers? And, as I suspect many interviewers of middle and high school students wonder, did I choose the right chips, cookies, fruit, juice, and soda to suit contemporary teenage tastes?

THE NEW YORK STUDENTS

The New York students had self-selected for the study and identified themselves as successful based on its criteria (outlined in the introduction), but teachers at the school reaffirmed the students' perceptions that these were among the most successful students at New York Global High School (NYGHS). All were planning to attend college, and their future plans ranged from cardiology to pediatrics to making "a lot of money" to send back home for "shoes and clothes." The students were primarily from Caribbean countries, Central America, and West Africa, plus one student from Bangladesh. All had been in the country for fewer than three years when they enrolled at the school, so no student in the group had been in the United States for longer than six years.

As the New York participants entered our un-airconditioned classroom on a hot day that previewed the summer to come, I also wondered if the heat and humidity would dampen their willingness to engage in conversation and if the six-foot-tall fan blaring in the corner of the room would be too loud for them to hear one another. Although students started the group conversations by answering questions with brief responses in a dutiful tone, this polite atmosphere changed as the conversation turned to topics such as teacher behavior (students echoed one another that some were respectful and helpful while others were dismissive of immigrant students), the low quality of school lunches (my snacks were appreciated), and memories of corporal punishment in their countries of origin.

The First Success Factor: Hard Work

I began by asking students to identify the factors that they believed contributed most to their success. As students considered one another's answers, they came to a consensus that "hard work" is the main attribute of a successful student at NYGHS. Charles, for example, said that in order to succeed he must "give [his] best in every class and never give up."[1] It is easy to imagine any high-achieving student making such a statement, but upon further discussion the students delved more deeply. They suggested that an adherence to hard work was particularly important for them and their immigrant peers, since there were many challenges and frustrations associated with being English-language learners that might otherwise lead students to give up. Berta explained the key to success for her and her peers:

> Work hard and never give up, because if we don't pass the Regents, we are feeling like it's the end of the world. So we have to think about it like we have another opportunity and be ready for the next time.

In Berta's statement, we hear hints of the specific challenges English-language learners can face in U.S. school contexts. The students agreed that many of their peers felt daunted by requirements such as the state Regents exams (required for graduation in New York) and were tempted to drop out rather than repeat these tests multiple times. For the successful students, an attitude of persistence in the face of challenges—accompanied by the support of teachers to put these challenges in perspective—was critical.

The Second Success Factor: Learning English

Not surprisingly given their circumstances as relatively recent immigrants, the students in the New York group concluded that learning

English was the second most important factor, after hard work, in what it took to be a successful student at NYGHS. They also saw English as key to their success in college and beyond. Classes at NYGHS are taught in English, but students often work in groups and are encouraged to use their native languages to translate for one another and to understand content, particularly at the ninth- and tenth-grade levels, when some students enter the school only a matter of weeks or even days after having immigrated to the U.S. There are a wide variety of native languages spoken at NYGHS, with Spanish being predominant. For this reason, some students even learned a third language (often French or Spanish) through their interactions with peers.

In addition to learning English at school, the students enjoyed talking about the different aspects of popular culture that helped them build their English skills. A number of them watched cartoons at home when they were first learning English and said that the simplicity and clarity of this form of entertainment helped them build their understanding gradually. Even as they debated what artists were best, several students agreed that the music of singers and rap artists—Alicia Keys, Lil Wayne, Rihanna, and others popular with U.S. teens—was also helpful in their efforts to build their English skills outside of school.

The Use of Native Languages with English

Although the students agreed that English was crucial to their success at school, they also agreed, virtually universally, that the use of their native languages was important, particularly when they were new to the country. As Omar, a West African student, explained, "When somebody just comes, they don't speak English, so they have to rely on people who speak the same language as they do to get their work done." Peers who could speak their native languages served as a lifeline for the students, but some students in the group also cautioned that there were pitfalls and limitations to this practice. As Ahmed, a student who immigrated from Bangladesh, explained, he felt frustrated—even as his same-language peers were helping him—when his ideas became "lost in translation":

When I came first time here, actually I knew everything [teachers were saying], but I can't say it because of language. There was another guy Bengali who knew more English than me and I tried to tell him, "I know the answer, can you tell him [the teacher]?" He just summarized what I said; he didn't tell everything.

Similarly, the students identified group work as a good opportunity to capitalize on the use of their original languages as well as English. They enjoy collaborating in the language in which they are most comfortable and said it made them feel successful when, as one student put it, "the whole group understands each other and understands the work." They added, however, that native-language collaboration sometimes becomes counterproductive when students use their native languages to get off task, or when such use might lead to the exclusion of a group member who speaks a different language than most other group members. As Ibrahim and Marco explained:

IBRAHIM: *It's sometimes important for [group members] not to understand each other. If there are people that speak Spanish and other people that speak another language, the Spanish-speaking people are going to be speaking to each other and the other people are going to be left out and not know what they're saying. They're not going to focus on work.*

MARCO: *When people speak the same language and come together, you're not focusing on your work. So when teachers try to make a group, they should think about putting students with different languages with each other.*

All the students enjoyed working with peers from different language backgrounds and said they had a diverse group of friends. As Omar explained, "I don't see who I'm not friends with at this school. Like in this school, it's Spanish, Africans, Arabs, everybody." Still, most admitted to retreating to same-language groupings in more social settings. Charles observed, "Like in the cafeteria, Africans always sit with Africans, Spanish always sit with Spanish, Arabs always sit with Arabs. Like, every kind of group always sits with each other." As he went on to

explain, same-language social groupings were based on common interests, comfort level with the language, and the need to find relief from
the "frustration" of speaking in English all the time during classes:

> *Since you're required to speak English [in class], you do your best to not*
> *speak Spanish or some other African language. But then when it comes*
> *to lunch, you just want a break from the frustration of speaking English,*
> *so you just go and sit with your people and talk in the language you're*
> *most comfortable with.*

New Expectations in Schooling

In addition to the adjustment associated with learning in a new language, students discussed the differences in expectations they perceived
between schools in their home countries and NYGHS. Students from
West African countries and the Dominican Republic said that there was
a heavy emphasis on memorization at their previous schools and that
they sometimes found this kind of work oppressive. In general, they enjoyed the interpretive work and critical thinking they were asked to do
at NYGHS, a school with a strong emphasis on portfolio-based assessment, whereby students are required to present aspects of what they
have learned to a panel. Learning in more student-centered ways, however, comes with adjustments, as Karla articulated. Although she said
she now enjoys the challenge of presenting her own work, she found
her first experience with portfolio-based presentations intimidating:

> *It was my first time to present portfolio, and I was crying. Now I think*
> *I'm better. I still feel challenged. Portfolio is very hard. You just need*
> *to be prepared and focus on what you're doing and what the teacher is*
> *teaching you.*

Students also discussed differences in the approaches to discipline
at schools in their home countries and at NYGHS. A number of them
mentioned corporal punishment as an oppressive aspect of their prior
schooling. As Ibrahim explained, at his school in West Africa, "You

had to memorize everything. The words you don't memorize, you get whipped." Echoing a sentiment expressed by several other students, however, he said he sometimes felt that teachers at NYGHS were too lax about discipline, and this affected students' motivation to excel:

> [At my previous school in Africa] if you talk and talk, and the teacher says you be quiet, that's it. . . . Here, all you got to do is just ignore the teacher and just keep talking. Nothing is going to happen. . . . In Africa, teachers have more power. Here, the students have more power than the teacher.

The Importance of Relationships with Teachers

In talking about their relationships with teachers, the immigrant students I met in New York were in many respects like any other group of high school students in that they had good relationships with some teachers and had relationships with other teachers that frustrated them or made them feel demoralized. Even though students in the group were academically successful, some felt particularly vulnerable as immigrant students and said that teachers were sometimes not as patient with them as they could be with regard to their understanding and use of English. Students nodded in agreement, for example, while their peers talked about teachers who pretended to understand them when they spoke English with accents instead of truly listening to find out what they were saying.

Nevertheless, virtually all students in the group had teachers they believed played a crucial role in their success at school. Among the factors students cited as particularly important in student-teacher relationships were longevity (often extending beyond a student's enrollment in a particular teacher's class); patience along with high expectations; and a willingness to listen to the student about a wide range of issues, both school-related and otherwise. Ahmed cited the importance of all these factors when talking about his relationships with three teachers:

To make a good relationship with the teacher is a matter of time. For example, when I came first time here, my English teacher was Ms. Marquita. Almost three years, I spent time with her. We make a good relationship with each other. . . .

I know the answer [in my chemistry class], but I don't talk because I don't feel confident. Because [the teacher's] new, and so I felt so shy. He asked me, he said, "Can you answer this question?" . . . So pushing the student also makes a good relationship.

I have a good relationship with the teacher named Mr. Jackson. We have a good relationship because whatever happened after school in my life, positive and negative, I share with him and he gives me some good advice.

The students saw a direct correlation between their relationships with teachers and their willingness to engage with the academic material in a particular teacher's class. Many said they met after school frequently with certain teachers and found them to be motivating and welcoming. Conversely, even these high-achieving students disengaged when they did not connect with a teacher or felt that the teacher disrespected them. As Omar explained:

When you feel connected to the teacher, you want to go to the class. It pushes you to listen to what he's saying . . . do good on tests and essays and everything. But if you don't care about the teacher, you just go, you don't listen, whatever he says, you're like, "I don't care." And when the time is over, you just get up and leave.

THE CALIFORNIA STUDENTS

Initial meetings with the California students took place after school on two subsequent days, the second of which was organized as an ice cream sundae–making party. As a younger group made up of primarily 1.5 generation immigrant youth who have been in the United States considerably longer than the New York students, the California students had somewhat different perspectives on the factors that help them succeed, while other issues they discussed echoed many raised by their New York counterparts. (According to Carola Suárez-Orozco, Desirée Baolian Qin, and Ramona Fruja Amthor, the 1.5 generation consists of young people who are "born abroad but arrive in their new homeland prior to the age of twelve.") Like the NYGHS students, all the Clarkson Community School (CCS) students were planning to attend college, but because they were younger, fewer of them had specific ideas about the fields they were planning to study. All of the students were born in Mexico, and the majority used Spanish as a primary language at home because one or both of their parents spoke little or no English. For some, their memories of schooling in Mexico were vague or nonexistent, while for others the difficulties of their transition to U.S. schooling were still fresh in their minds.

The First Success Factor: Parents

In California as in New York, numerous students stressed the importance of hard work and motivation as key factors in their success. Whereas most of the students in New York cited teachers as the individuals who most strongly motivated them and helped them succeed, students in the California focus group talked more about parents as key motivators. Some of this difference may obviously be attributed to the flow of focus group conversations (where one person's response sometimes influences another's) and to the fact that several students in the New York group had left parents behind in their countries of origin. Nevertheless, there was a common sentiment among the California group that students felt strongly motivated by their parents to rise above current family circumstances. A number of these students had parents who, as they put it, worked "in the fields," the kind of manual work common in California's farming areas that is physically demanding and low-paying. Others had parents who were restaurant servers or fruit stand clerks or worked in other relatively low-paying professions often held by Mexican immigrant adults in California. Several of these students said their diligence stemmed largely from their parents' encouragement and exhortations to work hard so that they would not have to work "in the fields" but might instead go to college and enjoy better-paying jobs. As Diana explained, "They [my parents] want me to be working in an office with, like, an air conditioner, that's what they tell me. With a heater, not over there in the fields where they work."

Parents thus play a significant role in the California students' motivation, and five of the nine named their mothers as the number-one support for their academic success—a statement that four of them then tellingly qualified by saying some version of "even though she doesn't know English." The "push" these students receive from their mothers takes different forms, ranging from homework help and taking them to school-related events to the loss of privileges if expectations are not met:

PEDRO: *I believe it's my mom [who is my primary support and motivator], because even though she doesn't know English, she'll try to help me on my homework.*

DIANA: *I would say my mom, because even though she doesn't know English, she's still there, she always tries to help me. . . . If I need to go somewhere related to school she is always there for me. She's always there for me no matter what.*

RICKY: *I would say my mom, because even though she doesn't know English . . . she always does what's best for me.*

LUIS: *I would say my mom, because she helped me succeed in my grades, like she made me raise them a little bit higher.*

JUAN: *I think it's my mom, even though she doesn't know much English, so she doesn't really help me. But, like, she threatens me, takes away my phone or something to make me, like, actually try hard.*

The Second Success Factor: Strong Relationships with Individual Teachers

Students in the California group were enthusiastic about CCS; when I asked them to indicate by show of hands how many liked the school, all hands went up. Students like the variety of offerings at the school and the opportunity to take classes in music and art, and upper-level students appreciate the opportunity to take college-level courses, especially since that might mean fewer college costs in the future for their families, many of whom are concerned about how they will pay for tuition. The students at CCS also said they appreciate the fact that they attend a small school where, as one student put it, "the staff and students mostly know everybody" and numerous staff members speak Spanish, which allows their parents to maintain active communication with educators. While some students were not happy about having to attend school from 8 a.m. to 5 p.m., the general consensus was that this schedule was both "good and bad," since, as one student whose parents do farmwork explained, "Some parents get off work late, and it makes it easier on them if they don't worry as much and they know exactly where we are." The only unanimous complaint was about the school uniform, the green polo shirts and khakis that Marisol said "make us look like trees."

The CCS students overall had positive things to say about most of their teachers, and along with strong parental motivation they cited positive relationships with teachers as important factors in their success. Like the New York students, the California students cited individual teachers as being especially influential in their lives, and the name of one math teacher, Ms. Alvarez, came up repeatedly in both the focus groups and the individual follow-up interviews as someone the students trusted and to whom they could talk not just about mathematics but about other things that were going on in their lives.

Eduardo was one of the California students who turned to teachers not only for help with schoolwork but for more personal advice as well. Eduardo said he wishes all teachers would "try to understand what's going on in our personal life as well, relate lessons to life . . . build relationships with us, instead of just, 'Go to page this, this, and this.'" Echoing other sentiments expressed by some of the students in the New York focus groups, however, Eduardo adds that not all teachers make an effort to form authentic relationships with students. He said some behave in a way that makes students feel dismissed and invisible: "They ignore you. They hear you and they see you, but they don't do anything."

The Use of Spanish with English

Because the California students had been in the United States considerably longer than those in New York, none of them felt the need to continue to use Spanish along with English to support their learning. Still, some recalled that in earlier grades, when they first arrived in the United States, some teachers helped them by translating lessons or concepts into Spanish—or by connecting them with students or other adults who could—while others discouraged them from using Spanish at all. As Diana explained, "I just remember that when I got here I didn't know any English, and the teachers weren't allowed to speak Spanish to you, and if the teachers caught you speaking in Spanish they got you in trouble."

Now the students in the CCS focus group, most of whom speak Spanish at home, speak English exclusively in class, except when socializing with their Spanish-speaking friends. In those cases, Marisol explained, she speaks Spanish "probably just like with your friends messing around. Like we mix it up—we're talking English, then go into Spanish." Daniela added that sometimes, "Like there's some words you can't remember in English or in Spanish, so you use the other language, and they understand you like that." And, as one might predict, the students also use Spanish at times "when you're trying to keep something from the teacher," as Eduardo admitted.

As fluent English speakers, students in the CCS group were more likely to use Spanish to help others than to seek help for themselves. As Pedro explained, "If it's a new kid that doesn't know English, you can help them out and talk to him in Spanish." In addition, some of the focus group students said they attend parent-teacher conferences with their parents and serve as translators, and they assist their parents and other family members with translation in public spaces outside of school.

Along with issues related to language, those students who had memories of having gone to school in Mexico cited other differences, such as the structure of the school day (for some, school ended in the early afternoon), how grade groupings akin to middle and high school were organized, and curriculum. As Daniela summed up, "Everything's different. . . . You're taught different history, Mexican history, you have different traditions—and there are no uniforms."

ADVICE TO TEACHERS

I ended both sets of group interviews by asking students to provide a short piece of advice to teachers for working effectively with them and their peers. They shared these responses in a round-robin format and, although there were some differences from one group to another, the word "patience" or some variation of it seemed to come up again and again. The New York students' advice included:

- "Consider the language."
- "Be patient."
- "[Remember that] different countries have different rules."
- "[Realize that] sometimes they think we know a lot of English like them."
- "Really listen."
- "Don't judge."

The California students offered advice such as:

- "Be patient, be okay with problems at home, and don't give up on them."
- "Help the person if it seems to be fair; have patience."
- "Understand the situation the student is having."
- "Don't wait for the students to ask for help—students may be embarrassed. Try to do something about it."
- "Be more patient with students who don't really care about school that much."
- "Go to their desk and ask for help."

Finally, Ahmed in New York offered advice that he said both immigrant students and their teachers should remember: "Nobody's perfect. Everybody should try their best."

HARD WORK—AND THE SUPPORT TO GET IT DONE

When listening to any group of high-achieving students, immigrant or otherwise, it is perhaps not surprising to hear them cite "hard work" as a primary factor contributing to their success. What the students in these two groups made clear, however, was that even if their diligent efforts are largely responsible for their academic achievement, they do not believe they are doing it alone.

Teachers—particularly special teachers—were mentioned again and again as making a crucial difference to students at critical points in their lives and in several important ways. When students were new to the United States, whether they were in the early elementary grades or in middle or high school, key teachers provided them with an entry point into what was otherwise a new and frightening world, either by translating class material into the students' native languages themselves or by connecting students with peers who could do it for them. After students became accustomed to working in English, they relied on special individual teachers both to motivate them academically and to serve as sounding boards for issues that might be taking place outside of school. Close relationships with key teachers have been found to be important factors in the positive development of all students, but they may have special significance for immigrant students who face language-related challenges, stresses that may be unique to their immigrant families, and other difficulties.[2]

The experiences of these young people suggest that immigrant students may need even more encouragement than U.S.-born adolescents to persist in pursuing their goals, since they can face considerable obstacles. In New York State, high school students who are English-language learners are required to take the state Regents exams even while they are still learning English and, in some cases, adjusting to the demands of being high school students for the first time. Moreover, when students are accustomed to education that emphasizes rote memorization, learning experiences that require them to draw upon higher-order thinking skills and previously untapped skills such as oral presentation (especially in a language that is new to them) can seem daunting.

In California, the highly motivated group of students I spoke with all planned to go to college, but they were worried about some of their less-motivated friends. Variations on phrases such as "my parents don't have much money," "they don't know much English," and "they don't have much education" were common refrains among the group. Although many students in the focus group cited high levels of emotional support and motivation from their families as clearly a strong asset, their comments also pointed to stresses and challenges among the families in this community that could have a significant impact on the students' ability to attend and succeed in college. The temptation to give up amid circumstances such as these, especially when they are combined with students' growing awareness of racism, anti-immigrant sentiments, and other obstacles they might experience upon graduation, can be considerable, as the high dropout statistics and low college attendance rates for students from immigrant families attest.[3] Nevertheless, the students in both groups consistently cited the work of teachers who were persistent, stuck with them even beyond the time they were enrolled in their classes, and provided a range of support, both academic and emotional.

We also hear in the comments of these successful students the value of additive approaches when students are new to the United States, in contrast to what researcher Angela Valenzuela has called "subtractive schooling," the attempt to "subtract" students' native languages and cultures when they come into U.S. schools.[4] While all the newly immigrated New York students placed learning English high on their list of assets for success, they also discussed the value of same-language groupings, both socially and academically, for helping them adjust to their new environment. Particularly in the earlier years of their U.S. schooling, students from both groups relied on same-language discussion with peers to understand academic content. Moreover, even as they mastered English, the students seem to have felt a need for what psychologist Beverly Daniel Tatum has called the "psychological safety" of their same-language peers, as a relief from the stress of working in English all day.[5] Their comments suggest a need for educators to balance both native-language and English-language work for newly immigrated students and to provide them with "safe space" and "escape" from the world of English from time to time, while simultaneously encouraging them to make cross-cultural friendships.

Overall, the students' comments illustrate how interconnected aspects of academic engagement, as Carola Suárez-Orozco and her colleagues noted in their research with immigrant students, can intersect in young people's lives and where one type of engagement can support another, contributing to better academic performance.[6] We hear evidence, for example, of how strong relationships with teachers and supportive relationships with peers (relational engagement) encourage students to perform the tasks of school with more enthusiasm (behavioral engagement). Conversely, however, we also hear evidence of students disengaging from teachers who they feel don't respect them, and situations in which disengagement in one area might contribute to disengagement elsewhere.

For the California students in particular, the role of parental support, motivation, and encouragement to succeed was striking, particularly in light of the perception among many teachers and school administrators that immigrant parents are uninvolved in their children's education.[7] If anything, the students' comments support prior research suggesting that immigrant parents are highly motivated to see their children succeed academically and go to college, and this motivation may be especially strong among Mexican immigrants who come to the United States as farmworkers.[8] For many of the students, this parental support seemed to complement support they received at school from both their teachers and their peers, suggesting the potential for these various aspects of the "ecologies" of children's lives to work in concert to support learning.[9]

PART TWO

The Portraits

Omar

"There are some people, they listen, but they don't know what you're talking about. And there's other people you talk to, they'll really listen."

A Network of Relationships, Carefully Chosen

AT AGE NINETEEN, Omar is one of the oldest students I interviewed for *Portraits of Promise*, and in both the focus group and individual interviews he projected an air of thoughtful and confident maturity.[1] Four years prior to his interview, Omar moved to the United States from Burkina Faso, a country in West Africa. He came to New York at age fifteen with his mother and his five-year-old sister knowing only Mòoré, a regional language of Burkina Faso, and French, the "official" European language there. Omar was a good student in his native country and had begun to take college-level courses there. He was then thrust into an

American high school knowing virtually no English and little about what was expected of him in this new context:

> *Like, when you go to a new school, of course you're going to be, like, frustrated. You don't know a lot of people, and especially the language. Like, the hardest thing is you're just sitting there staring at the teacher, they're talking and you don't know what they're saying. So you just got to sit there, look at whatever they're doing. You can't even read whatever the person is writing on the board, so it's hard.*

Nearing the end of his senior year at New York Global High School (NYGHS), Omar has completed all of his state Regents exams successfully. He received a score of 76 on the English language arts Regents test (which English language learners are required to take in English) and a 98 on the U.S. history exam, the highest in the history of NYGHS. He also has recently been accepted to one of the city's community colleges for fall admission. During lunch and after school, Omar can often be seen in the classroom of a teacher who runs an informal chess club, of which Omar is one of the most regular members. He now speaks English almost exclusively at school (except for occasional lunch conversations with the four other Mòoré speakers at NYGHS), and he sees continual improvement in English as a key to his future success:

> *When I'm at school, I use only English and that's it. Even French, we don't speak French, like, over here. The more you speak English, the better you get at it, so I speak English with my friends to make sure I improve my English, the vocabulary and everything.*

When I ask Omar to reflect on the factors that helped him past his initial feelings of alienation and confusion when he first arrived at NYGHS, he explains that even as a new student, he recognized that he needed to seek help from as many sources as possible. This would then allow him to evaluate which relationships would be most beneficial to him over the long term and to invest more energy in cultivating these relationships:

When I came [to NYGHS], I went to everybody. When I have some-thing [like a question or problem], I'll go to you. I'll go to this person tomorrow, I'll go to this person next week, see who communicates better with me. Who answers my question the way I want it answered? Who doesn't just—somebody who doesn't just listen and nod, just staring at me, like a person who doesn't know what I'm talking about. Because there are some people, they listen, but they don't know what you're talking about. And there's other people you talk to, they'll really listen. They actually, like, talk to you when you're talking, give you advice on what to do and not to do.

Echoing a theme heard in other interviews as well as in the focus groups, Omar draws a distinction here between teachers who "really listen" and those who only pretend to do so. In the New York focus groups, several students talked about feeling that, because they were immigrant students and spoke English imperfectly and with accents, some teachers didn't take them or their ideas seriously—those who might, as Omar says, "nod, just staring at me, like a person who doesn't know what I'm talking about."

Over the course of his four years at NYGHS, Omar says he has thus developed the skill of figuring out which teachers have a sincere interest in him and truly believe that he can achieve at a high level and which have a more patronizing attitude. Omar says he now has excel-lent relationships with two adults in particular at school, his English teacher and a school counselor. In the same way that these kinds of relationships were significant for many other students in the study, the willingness of these educators to talk about issues not related to school is particularly important to Omar:

I can say my English teacher, Ms. Sheila, and Ms. Marie [a counselor], the two of them, they really help me a lot. Because whenever I'm stuck with something or have problems outside the school and need to talk to somebody, they're always there to answer my questions, help me with problems I have, give me advice on what to do and what not to do. I would say that they help me the most.

Another adult relationship that Omar says has been especially meaningful for him has been one he formed through a formal mentoring program, City Match, that pairs recent college graduates with adolescents from low-income parts of the city. Here, he says, the focus was not on academics but on doing "fun things" with his mentor through which he learned to "get his mind relaxed" and ultimately do better in school:

> *[One of the best things] I would say this year, at the beginning of the year, they were having some program where they give everybody a mentor. Like on Saturdays you meet up with your mentor, and you, like, do things to get your mind relaxed: jogging, bike riding, bowling, anything to just get you to do fun things and not focus all your time on school.*
>
> *[Otherwise], Saturdays, you just stay home, sometimes they give you homework, you watch TV, and that's it. So I really liked going out with them [the mentors and mentees], because sometimes we'd go bowling, sometimes you go to the park, Central Park, we'd go there and we'd, like, do fun things.*

A HIGH LEVEL OF RESPONSIBILITY

One of the things Omar's mentoring program seems to have provided for him was a release from responsibility, apparently a significant factor across several aspects of his life. When I ask Omar whether he feels a great deal of responsibility to do well, he says that he does and that much of this is centered around family:

> *Of course, because they're [my family is] always expecting me to do better than they did. So I got to always do my best—and care for my sister. Everyday I finish here, I gotta go straight to the babysitter, get my sister, and go home.*

As the oldest child in his family, Omar takes on a great deal of the care for his five-year-old sister while his mother works evenings as a security guard. (His father is still living in Africa, but Omar says he plans to move to the States in the next few years.) Although a very diligent student, Omar says he spends only about thirty minutes per night on homework because of his other duties at home:

> *Once I get home, I gotta feed my sister, help her do her homework and everything, like. Because I feed her, help her do homework, whatever, take a shower. Then after that—that probably takes about four to five hours—then after that I go take my shower, eat, then do my homework.*

DIFFERENCES IN AFRICAN AND AMERICAN LIFE

Despite the great responsibility Omar feels, both to do well because of his family's sacrifices and to care for his young sister, he enjoys living in the United States and believes it offers him and his family opportunities that they would not have if they had stayed in Burkina Faso. Even with some of the challenges he has already faced, Omar seems to have maintained a sense of possibility for his life in the U.S. and is optimistic about the future, and NYGHS seems to have played a role in his feeling connected to American society:

> *Here [in the United States] you can do whatever you want to do. . . . You come here, you get the opportunity to get a good job. As long as you work hard, you get what you want.*
>
> *Life is good there [in Burkina Faso], but one problem is there's not a lot of money there. You go to school, you get your diploma and everything, and you're stuck without a job. . . . Here, if you get a diploma, probably the longest you would stay without a job is a month or two.*
>
> *I think the one thing I like most about living in the States is that we communicate with each other. Not everybody is friends with each other, but when you're in a community like this school everybody talks to each other—everybody's friendly and likes each other—no racism, nothing. I don't know if everywhere in the country it's like that, but where I am right now I like where I am.*

Next, I ask Omar if there is anything he does not like about living in the United States as compared to Burkina Faso. His answer is similar to that given by several of the other New York students and is one that many urban high school students, whether immigrant or U.S.-born, might echo—he does not always feel safe on the street. Omar's response, however, also reflects another perception found among some immigrant black students—that there is an adversarial relationship between him (and other immigrant students from Africa, the Caribbean, and elsewhere) and black students born in the United States:

> The thing I don't like is that sometimes the streets are not safe. . . . Black Americans are always looking at you—like, if you have something good on you, they sometimes try to take it. So you always gotta be on the lookout walking. Even make sure you're walking with your friends and not walking alone, like at night. It's always dangerous. In my country, when you're walking and people see something they like, that doesn't happen. You can walk whatever time you want. There's no problem with that, because everybody—like there's no harm walking. Like, if somebody sees you, they don't try to have a fight with you.

In addition to the risk of getting "jumped" or being the victim of theft (mostly of personal electronics such as cell phones and iPods), there has been gang activity in the neighborhood around NYGHS. On occasion, NYGHS administrators have counseled students to avoid certain streets near the school where rashes of crime have taken place. Omar says he has avoided gang involvement and other forms of trouble by heeding the advice of school officials and through the careful choice of his friends:

> The people I hang out with, I make sure they're not in gangs. Because once you hang out with a person that's in gangs, one day they're going to ask you to come and chill with their friends. And once you go, you might become part of the gang.
>
> My friends, some of them hang out with gang people, so whenever they tell me, "Come hang out with me," I'm like, "No, I'm good." So

when they finish their business over there, we can chill. That's what I like. But I'm not going to go with you and do whatever y'all are doing over there, gang stuff. I don't even know whatever y'all are doing there, and I don't want to know.

Another key difference between life in New York and in Burkina Faso, according to Omar, relates to school discipline. Reiterating opinions shared in the focus groups, Omar believes his teachers in New York have considerably less control over students than did his teachers in Africa. Because the teachers in Burkina Faso sometimes used corporal punishment, Omar does not necessarily believe that their approaches to discipline were better, but he does question whether the teachers at NYGHS motivate students as strongly as they could:

Here, the difference is they don't really force you to do the work. They give you the work—you want to do it, they help you do it. You don't want to do it, that's you. But in Africa, there's no "I'm going to do it, or I don't want to do it." You are obligated to do it. You don't do it, they'll, like, punish you—that's the thing, so you're going to do it. . . . They use some whips and everything, they got boards, like they hit your hand with it, anything to get you to do the work. . . . They use any, like, form of punishment possible, not severe, but anything to get you to do the work.

OMAR'S PREPARATION FOR THE FUTURE

An avid chess player and a successful math and science student, Omar hopes to work in the high-tech industry in the future, but this plan differs from his mother's wishes for him: "I'm thinking about becoming a computer specialist, I think. That's what I'm thinking about, but my mom is talking about me going into medical studies or something."

Having already been accepted to one of the best community colleges in the city, after which he will probably transfer to a four-year college, Omar says he feels well prepared for the future and especially for working with others. This skill is cultivated on a virtually daily basis at

NYGHS, where in most classes students sit at work tables of four to six students and collaborate throughout the class. In the lower grades, many of these groupings are monolingual so that students can translate for each other and learn in both English and their native languages. At the upper level, many groupings are cross-cultural, a dynamic that Omar believes provides especially good preparation for his future:

> *In high school, they say, like, when you get a job it's all about group work, everything is group work. You gotta be able to communicate with your co-workers, with others, work together to get something done. So I think here they challenge us to work in groups . . . talk to each other, get the work done, even though you're not familiar with the people.*
>
> *One time I had a job and I didn't know anybody there, but since I already knew how to work in groups, I was able to participate and do my part of the work so that everybody can, so that we can get the job done.*

Omar believes that these collaborative skills, as well as a strong work ethic and his willingness to ask for help whenever he needs it, are (at least in his case) more important than innate intelligence. When I ask him if he believes he is smart, he responds:

> *I wouldn't say I'm smart, but I'm in the middle. I'm okay. I think I'm okay. . . . My mom graduated from high school and she knows some of the things I do, so she helps with homework. Sometimes I call friends to help me, and other times I just leave it until I get to school and ask the teacher.*

Omar is strongly connected to his African heritage and says he considers himself more African than American because "that's where I was born and raised, and that's where I learned everything I needed to know." Since Omar sees advantages to life both in the United States and in Burkina Faso, however, he is unsure whether, when he completes his studies, he would like to stay in the U.S. or go back to Africa. His current solution to this dilemma is to imagine having a home in both countries. When I ask him if he would like to return to Burkina Faso as an adult, he says:

> *I would say not, like, forever. But I don't want to stay here forever either. Going back and forth. I'll have a house there, maybe I'll have a house here.*

In any case, Omar is similar to many of the other immigrant students profiled in this book in that helping people in his home country is an important part of his future plan, whether he lives in Burkina Faso again or stays in the United States. Omar explains that his mother shares this wish for his future, and he believes the work of his teachers at NYGHS will also help him to achieve this objective in the end:

> *What [my mother] wants for me is to graduate from high school, then college, get a good job, help my people. . . . Back in my country, it's kind of a poor country, so it's not every day that people get to eat. So she wants me to get a good job and help my people back there, like my family members. And that's basically what the school is trying to do, too. All they want is for you to graduate, go to college, and get a job. So it's all working in the same direction.*

LISTENING TO OMAR

Omar's experience speaks to the initial disorientation many immigrant students feel upon their arrival in U.S. schools, even if they have already experienced a high level of success as students in their countries of origin.[2] Due to some combination of maturity and self-confidence, Omar seems to have navigated the new world of NYGHS with a savvy awareness of what relationships could be most beneficial to him as well as a sense of self-advocacy. He has succeeded by seeking out those who see him for the intelligent young adult he is and provide the most valuable assistance while, conversely, investing less effort in relationships where teachers and others seem dismissive or otherwise unhelpful. Echoing what other immigrant students, both in this project and in prior research, have said about teachers who are willing to help students beyond academics, Omar believes the teachers who have been most important to his success are those to whom he can go "whenever I'm stuck with something or have problems outside the school . . . [who are] always there to answer my questions."[3] Omar's story thus illustrates the way relational engagement with teachers can contribute to a student's behavioral engagement in school, their enthusiasm and willingness to engage in schoolwork and related tasks.[4]

In addition to teachers, Omar's positive experience with the City Match mentoring program speaks to the value of high-quality relationships with adults for immigrant youth, not just to help them with schoolwork but to provide social outlets that contribute to a greater sense of belonging. The mentoring program with which Omar was involved, in which he enjoyed activities ranging from bowling to trips to Central Park, places special emphasis on exposing students to the variety of experiences available in New York City, thus helping them to acclimate not only to the immediate surroundings in their school's neighborhood (which, in Omar's case, he experienced as somewhat violent) but to a rich array of experiences. As many adolescent development theorists have noted, exposure to a variety of experiences can lead to an enhanced sense of possibility for a young person, immigrant or otherwise.[5]

Omar's description of his family's wishes for his future, particularly his mother's desire that he become a doctor, are illustrative of the hopes that many immigrant parents have for their children, especially those who show exceptional academic promise. Being fourteen years older than his sister, however, Omar is typical of many immigrant youth who have a level of responsibility at home that is higher than what most U.S.-born high school students experience.[6] This situation is exacerbated by the fact that Omar lives with a single mother who works long hours to support the family, and he therefore assumes much of the caregiving responsibility for his five-year-old sister. As researcher and educator Tamara Lucas and her colleagues have noted, the increased responsibilities that some immigrant students face at home can cause conflict at school if teachers are not aware of these circumstances and the burden they may place on a student's demeanor in class or ability to complete work on time.[7] Omar's home situation appears to have done little to diminish his academic success (with his 98 score on the U.S. history Regents exam being only one such example), but it nevertheless speaks to the need for educators to know about the home environments of their immigrant students, particularly in cases where they may be taking on considerable responsibility outside of school.

In addition to his family, Omar seems to feel a strong connection to Burkina Faso and a desire to "help my people" after he completes his education, illustrating the connection that many immigrant students feel to their countries of origin even as they value their new life in the United States.[8] Omar clearly feels a sense of community at NYGHS in ways that cross boundaries of culture and language that might be more rigid in other schools: "Not everybody is friends each other, but when you're in a community like this school everybody talks to each other everybody's friendly and likes each other—no racism, nothing." Also, as he said in the focus groups, "I don't see who I'm not friends with at this school. Like in this school, it's Spanish, Africans, Arabs, everybody." Other students from NYGHS spoke to a similar sense of cross-cultural community in their interviews, and a discussion of the school context in this regard is included in the concluding chapter. Omar's perception of a lack of safety in the neighborhood outside the school (discussed in more detail in the portrait of Ibrahim), however, points to the risks facing many immigrant students who attend schools in major cities, especially since the majority of schools serving large concentrations of immigrant students are located in neighborhoods where street crime is a constant threat as they travel to and from school.[9]

Moreover, Omar's comments suggesting his distrust of "Black Americans" illustrate a need for educators to pay attention not only to the relationships among different groups of immigrant students in their schools but also to the interactions that take place, both inside and outside school, between immigrant youth and those born in the U.S. Omar's negative personal experiences in the neighborhoods surrounding the school have clearly played a role in shaping his opinions. His comments therefore point to the need for educators to engage immigrant students in critical conversations about issues such as prejudice, stereotypes, and racism so that they can put their experiences with other youth in proper perspective.

Diana

*"I wasn't going to let them tell me
what I was capable of."*

Thriving Through Resistance

DIANA IS A SOFT-SPOKEN, polite, and—by her teachers' accounts—respectful fourteen-year-old student at California's Clarkson Community School. Although she shared openly, if quietly, several times in the initial focus group interviews, she ceded the floor on most questions to her more talkative classmates. When I reviewed Diana's transcript after the focus groups, I was somewhat surprised to see her extremely high achievement level, given her relatively deferential behavior among her peers. Her consistent straight-A grades read like those of a successful applicant to an Ivy League college. In fact, Diana has her sights set on one of the Ivies (she's not sure which one yet) after graduation from Clarkson, even though she is only in her freshman year, and her grades suggest that goal might be a real possibility. When I ask Diana whether she thinks she has an intellectual gift, at first she seems embarrassed by the question and reluctant to talk about her own abilities, but eventually she shyly responds, "That's what people tell me."

DIANA'S TRANSITION TO U.S. SCHOOLING

Born in a small city in Mexico, Diana had started school at an early age because she showed exceptional promise. She then immigrated to the United States with her parents, sister, and three brothers when she was five. When Diana first arrived in the U.S., she knew no English and entered school feeling confused, frightened, and homesick:

> I didn't want to be here. I didn't. I just wanted to go back. It was really difficult for me. I remember when I was small I used to love school. I wasn't supposed to be in school yet, but my mom knew the teacher, and she went and talked to them and, like in Mexico, because you're supposed to be, I think, six to be in school. . . .
>
> But then when I moved here I started first grade, so it was really difficult for me. I already knew, like, my ABCs and stuff, but in Spanish. And then when I got here the teachers couldn't, like, speak to you in Spanish, and they would get me in trouble if I spoke it. So it was really difficult for me.

In addition to the challenge of learning a new language, Diana says the behavior and attitudes of her classmates in the U.S. made for an extremely difficult transition. Her first teacher in the U.S. allowed other students to ostracize and make fun of her, and this teacher even contributed to Diana's feelings of marginalization by communicating racist and anti-immigrant attitudes that Diana says at first left her feeling alone and hopeless:

> I couldn't talk to the other girls, I couldn't talk to, like, people because like I didn't know English. People, like, they would make fun of me. They would tell me a lot of stuff . . . like I was stupid, like a lot of stuff.
>
> I had a teacher and she used to tell me that, too. She was like, I don't know—I think just because I was Mexican she thought I was incapable of what other, white people could do. . . . She didn't want to speak Spanish, and then she would like make it harder on me, like she

would tell me that I wasn't supposed to be there because I didn't know English—like, that I would have to take kinder [kindergarten] again and that I wasn't going to move higher up.

Through her mother's advocacy, Diana was removed from her initial teacher's class and into a first-grade classroom taught by a male teacher who believed in her talent and worked with her in both Spanish and English. This teacher tutored Diana after school and, as she says, "put in hours to help me understand," giving her the extra time and instruction she needed to apply her academic skills in a new language:

> *So my mom changed me out of that [first teacher's] class, and I got a really good teacher, and he would help me in Spanish. He would tell my mom, "You know what? She's higher up in level than, like, other students are that actually do know English." And then, like, [at first] I would go and tell my mom I didn't want to go there, I just didn't want to be in school. So, like, she told me to just sit there and just listen and I would learn it eventually—that if I didn't want to say anything and I didn't want to do anything I didn't have to. And the teacher told me the same thing. . . . And eventually I started learning English. . . .*
>
> *My [new] teacher, he really helped me. He really helped me understand. He used to give me tutoring, like, after school, and it was like only me, and then he would try to teach me English better, and by second grade, my second-grade year I already understood a lot. . . . I think it was because that teacher put in extra hours to help me understand.*

With patience and help, Diana's first-grade teacher allowed her the time and space to learn both English and class content (and class content *in* English) at her own pace, and his efforts made a clear and lasting impression on her: "After I went to second grade, he stopped teaching. But I will always remember him."

Diana's early years of schooling were thus the source of considerable stress for her, and it is easy to imagine a student in her circumstances giving up were it not for the efforts of a teacher who reached out to her and saw her promise. Yet Diana says that even the most difficult experiences she had in her early transition to U.S. schooling have motivated her to excel. In recalling her experiences with the unsupportive kindergarten teacher, Diana becomes emotional, describing how the teacher's behavior angered her but at the same time fueled a determination to prove that the teacher and others who might doubt her ability were wrong (my question in bold):

> I didn't think she believed in me, and then later on I used that. I was like, "I'm not going to let people tell me, like, what I'm capable of." So, like, I use that, and I'm doing better than most kids right now.
>
> **How do you think you use those experiences as fuel to motivate you, or is it just something inside you?**
>
> Maybe because I was really angry at people and I really, like, I wasn't going to let them tell me what I was capable of. . . . (Begins to cry.) Sorry. . . . Just because I kept this to myself a long time, and I try to forget it but it's like, that's what I remember. And, like, [I would see this happening to] other kids and, like, I kind of know what they went through.

For Diana, even though her traumatic early U.S. schooling experiences are a fresh source of emotion for her, her ability to "use" these memories, and perhaps even her anger about what transpired, seem paradoxically to serve as assets that contribute to her continued success as a student. In addition, these experiences have given her a sense of empathy for other students who have similar experiences and frustrations.

COMPLEMENTARY FAMILY- AND SCHOOL-BASED SUPPORT

In the story of Diana's early years of schooling, her mother plays several key roles. When Diana's mother saw that she was ready for school in Mexico even though she was younger than the required age to begin kindergarten, she advocated successfully for Diana to start school a year early. Similarly, when Diana began her U.S. schooling experiences with a teacher who was clearly unsupportive and held racist and anti-immigrant views, her mother switched her to a class with a teacher who saw her potential and was willing to work with her in Spanish and English to realize it:

> *I told my mom I didn't want to be there [in the first teacher's class]. I didn't want that teacher, and she moved me out. My mom has always been supporting me since the beginning. I remember one time [the teacher] told me that I was going to be like every other person there, that I was going to be working in the fields, that I wasn't, like, going to be anything. And I told my mom, and that's when my mom said, "You're going to go to college."*

When Diana was in middle school and her parents heard about Clarkson Community School, they thought it might provide her with a more rigorous education than she was getting in her traditional public school and asked her if she wanted to attend CCS. Despite the fact that neither of Diana's parents speak English and are thus unable to help her in any specific way with her schoolwork, Diana continues to view them as her primary motivators:

> *They're always there, they're always helping me. And they try to motivate me. They don't accept anything lower than an A, and if I get an A-minus, they're still there saying you needed an A, an A!*

Diana's parents—her father is a farmworker and her mother has stopped working to raise the children—exemplify a phenomenon common among immigrant parents. While instilling deeply held values of hard work and self-respect, these parents also want their children to work in vastly different circumstances from those in which they often find themselves. For parents in the area surrounding CCS, this often translates to working "in the fields," low-paying, difficult labor at one or more of the agricultural companies in the area. Diana is clearly motivated and emotionally moved by her parents' hard work, the sacrifices they have made for the family, and their support and expectations for her despite their own difficult circumstances:

> *I want to be as hard-working as them and follow in their footsteps. They couldn't do what they wanted to do because they didn't have the educa-tion, they didn't have the money. . . . I want to be the first one to go to college. That's what my mom wanted, but she couldn't make it; she didn't have the money. But, like, I try to, like, do what they couldn't do.*

When I ask Diana whether it is difficult to live up to her parents' high expectations for her, she says it is "sometimes difficult because you have to be a role model to your brothers and sisters." In general, however, Diana shares her parents' goal of her being the first family member to attend college, and she highlights the complementary role that teachers play in spurring on her success toward this goal. While Diana shares with me that it took her a long time to trust teachers in the U.S. because of her experience in kindergarten ("I was a little girl, and the person I looked up to was my teacher, and she used to tell me all this [negative] stuff."), she now believes that her teachers at CCS provide her with valuable help on two levels, both academic and personal:

> *I think if you have a good relationship with your teachers and you have your own motivation, not only your parents', it's not as difficult as people say [to be a successful student]. . . .*
>
> *My math teacher, I really like her. She's always asking if you need help, even if the student doesn't go up to her. She always goes around and she understands that someone might be shy. Like my Spanish teacher, I have a really good relationship with her; I think that, like, if I have a problem, I could just go to her and, like, she'd try to help me solve it.*

Another way in which Diana's teachers at Clarkson help her in ways that her parents are unable to is in navigating the transition to college, which she has begun to contemplate. In addition to SAT prepa-ration, workshops on the college application process, and college-level courses for students in the upper grades, the credits from which are accepted at many colleges, CCS educators have taken students to a local college fair, which Diana, even as a ninth-grader, had recently attended. Diana believes that Clarkson "pushes you in a way that other schools don't."

Thus, Diana sees her family and her school working in a concerted way to move her toward realizing her goals. When I ask her whether she sees any differences or conflict between the school's values and her parents', Diana says:

> *I think my parents expect the best out of me, and that's what the school expects out of you, too. Like, they expect you to go to college, they want you to go to college. There is actually no difference, because your parents want the best for you, and the school tries to help you out as much as they can.*

Ultimately, however, now that Diana is a teenager, she seems to have internalized the support from both her family and school and sees her own determination as a third critical factor in her success:

> *You can have an A or an A-plus if you want, but you have to have your own determination; people can't just be out there pushing you. Because if you don't want to, even if you have a lot of people there for you, you're still not going to make it. People need to have their own determination and believe in themselves.*
>
> *It's good to have people pushing you and it's good to have people that care about you, because it feels good to have someone there for you, but they're not going to be the one who's going to get the A for you.*

PREPARING FOR A FUTURE OF SERVICE TO OTHERS

When I ask Diana to tell me how she envisions her life as an adult, she shares with me her goal of becoming a pediatrician and discusses this aspiration in the context of the doubts some expressed in her early childhood that she could aspire to a high-level profession:

I see myself as a pediatrician. I don't know. I want to help people; that's what I want to do. I just like kids; I like working with kids, and I see myself doing the things that people told me I never could.

In addition to the math and science courses in which Diana excels, she has participated in numerous interscholastic science fairs and mathematics competitions. On weekends, she works as a volunteer at a senior residence, serving meals and providing companionship to older adults, many of whom she says have few visitors. While she says she is "not really into sports," she participates in community service and fundraising activities through her school's Key Club. There is thus a strong thread of service to others that runs through both Diana's current involvements and her future goals. While it is impossible even for her to speculate about the reasons for this focus, it seems that her early experiences of marginalization—as well as the help and support she received from key people at critical points in her life—may have helped her at a relatively young age to empathize with the needs of other people and to make this a central aspect of her life: "I want to do something not just for myself but for others."

Diana is unsure whether she would like to practice medicine in the United States or in Mexico. She says she "loves Mexico" and is looking forward to being able to visit her grandparents and other relatives there in the next year, but she also believes there may be more opportunities for her in the U.S. after she receives her medical training:

Most of my family's over there [in Mexico]; I don't really have family here, so that makes it harder. . . .

I tell them [my family] that when I get a job I'll go live in Mexico, but I don't know—maybe, maybe not. It's just—I don't know. Maybe I'll bring my grandparents over here instead. I don't know. I just, like, I don't really know what my future is. . . .

Although Diana does not identify politically as Chicana (she seemed unfamiliar with this concept when I brought it up), she is clearly resistant to stereotypes about Mexicans and Mexican Americans, as is evident both in her own educational history and her beliefs about how American society needs to change.[1] She ends our one-on-one interview by sharing with me her determination to demonstrate to the world that the anti-Mexican or anti-immigrant beliefs that some people in the United States hold should not and will not define her destiny:

> *I think it's going to be hard on Mexicans [in the future], and it is. It's just like—they [others] don't really understand what you go through. People should be more open. They need to understand that it's hard for you and try to help you out as much as possible. That's what I think. People should be more open-minded and all that. . . . My determination is to show people I'm Mexican. Like, so what? I wasn't born here. That doesn't matter.*

LISTENING TO DIANA

Like Omar and many other students profiled in other research, Diana experienced an initial state of extreme disorientation upon attending school in the United States for the first time, but her transition took place at a much younger age than Omar's.[2] Also, in contrast to the welcoming sense of community Omar experienced at NYGHS, Diana's early days of schooling in the U.S. were characterized by hostility and low expectations about her ability both from peers and from teachers. As researcher Evangeline Harris Stefanakis has noted, young immigrant children are disproportionately likely to be labeled with "special needs" by educators who are unable to see their academic potential through their limited initial proficiency in English.[3] In Diana's case, teachers' low expectations for her were both academically and emotionally damaging because, as she recalls, they were motivated in part by racist and anti-immigrant attitudes: "I think just because I was Mexican she thought I was incapable of what other, white people could do." Fortunately for Diana, in keeping with a theme that recurred throughout these interviews, the efforts of a "special teacher" seem to have turned the tide for her academically during the early grades. Like other students in these interviews, Diana notes that the willingness of this teacher to put in extra time, particularly to help her understand content in English, made a lasting impression that remains meaningful to her years later: "After I went to second grade, he stopped teaching. But I will always remember him."

Through the efforts of the teacher who believed in her ability and allowed her the time and space to learn content in English, Diana began to thrive academically. Ironically, however, her story suggests that her first U.S. teacher, who doubted her ability and potential, as well as the peers who initially ostracized her, also played unwitting roles in her success. Following these negative experiences, Diana seems to have built up a well of resistance that fueled her motivation to succeed. In her work studying the issues affecting African American girls, scholar Janie Victoria Ward defines resistance as "the development of a critical consciousness that is invoked to counter the myriad distortions, mistruths, and misinformation perpetrated about the lives of black women and men, their families, and communities."[4] Although Ward was writing primarily about African American communities, her definition seems applicable to Diana and her response to the "distortions, mistruths, and misinformation" she received about herself and about Mexicans and Mexican Americans during her early years of elementary school. Even as a young child, Diana seems to have developed a "critical consciousness" about the attitudes to which she was subjected that has motivated her all the way to the present day, in which she now has a straight-A transcript. Looked at another way, Diana's attitude could be viewed as an example of what researchers of successful African American males have called the "prove-them-wrong syndrome," a strong motivation to succeed in the face of stereotypes about one's social group.[5]

In addition to the first-grade teacher who believed in her abilities and helped her succeed, Diana seems to have built up this personal well of resistance through the support, encouragement, and advocacy of her family, especially her mother. When Diana told her mother about her first-grade teacher's unsupportive and racist attitude, Diana says her mother took immediate action: ". . . [T]hat's when my mom said, 'You're going to college.'" Diana's mother has also served as a key advocate for her at other points in her schooling career: getting her started in kindergarten in Mexico a year early; encouraging her to attend CCS; and insisting that, even when she is doing well, she aim higher: "You need an A, an A!" (Issues surrounding the encouragement and advocacy of immigrant parents are discussed in more detail in the next portrait.)

With her sights now set on an Ivy League college, Diana seems to be thriving by drawing on the same well of resistance she developed in elementary school and through the help and advocacy of her family and her teachers. Understandably, Diana says it took her time to learn to trust teachers in the U.S. after her initial experiences, but she now benefits not only from her day-to-day work in the classroom but from special events such as college fair field trips, organized by the educators at school, that allow her to think about what lies ahead. Like other students who participated in this study and feel strong emotional ties to their countries of origin, Diana says she still "loves Mexico" but is unsure about whether she will return there after her studies are completed. Also like many of her *Portraits of Promise* counterparts, Diana's goals for the future involve not only financial success but helping others through a career that serves society. She is one of three young women in these eight profiles whose goal is to become a pediatrician because, as she puts it, "I want to do something not just for myself but for others."

Ricky

"My parents had a very hard life when they were small, and they're always saying how hard it was, how hard it is in the fields, and that they expect me to go to college and get a good job."

The Power of Parents

RICKY IS IN MANY RESPECTS an exceptional twelve-year-old. His straight-A transcript aside, Ricky presents himself as mature and thoughtful in one-on-one conversations with adults while still being an approachable and well-liked seventh-grader who fits in easily among his peers. While observing Ricky's history class at CCS, I saw him code-switch adeptly between being "one of the guys" in the early stages of a small-group project and, once it came time to present the group's findings, a student leader on whose guidance his peers relied to put their best foot forward. As a highly successful student, Ricky is thus able to avoid drawing attention to himself as a "nerd" but instead wears his success in such a way that his classmates feel comfortable both being his friend and drawing on him as a resource when they need help.

Despite the fact that he is still in middle school, Ricky has already begun thinking in specific terms about college and has his sights set on Stanford, Caltech, or UC–San Diego to study biochemistry (a field that two of his cousins practice in Mexico). He seems already somewhat savvy about the college application process, and when I told him that a press associated with Harvard was publishing this book, he asked if I could use his real name in his portrait. (He understood when I explained the need to use pseudonyms in research to protect human subjects, but I told him he was free to reveal his identity to admissions officers at any college where he might apply.) Ricky is also already aware of scholarship programs that exist to help students from low-income families afford college, which he says will be important for him because "my family doesn't have much money."

A FIRM FOUNDATION OF FAMILY SUPPORT

Ricky immigrated to California with his parents and four siblings when he was four years old. Although Ricky is very much an American high school student (his history teacher was surprised to learn that he was not born in the United States), his home life very much reflects the experience of an immigrant family. Ricky says he speaks Spanish about 90 percent of the time at home and that his family struggles in ways that are common among immigrant families living and working in California's agricultural communities. While his mother stays home to care for his younger siblings, his father, Ricky says, "works in the fields," not for any particular company but wherever work is available at any given time. Ricky's parents are like those heading many immigrant families in that, despite their own challenges, they are fiercely driven to help their children rise above their own circumstances. As Ricky explains:

> My parents had a very hard life when they were small, and they're always saying how hard it was, how hard it is in the fields, and that they expect me to go to college and get a good job.

In fact, Ricky cites his parents as the strongest contributing factor (in addition to his own hard work) to his success as a student. Even though they are not able to help him much with his schoolwork because they speak little English, Ricky says his parents find myriad ways to support him toward the goals he has for college and beyond:

> *My parents always do whatever they can to help me out, whether it's buy[ing] me something important. Like, I like participating in science fairs, so they buy me all the materials I need. If they need to transport me somewhere, like to a college tour or like field trips, they always, like, take me.*

Ricky adds, however, that he does not find this level of parental support to be universal among his friends. Although most of the students in the *Portraits of Promise* study have outstanding grades, one of the things students in the California focus group shared was that they had plenty of peers whom they viewed as academically at risk, and Ricky believes that the attitudes and actions of his parents make a critical difference in his ability to rise above the pitfalls to which these students are vulnerable:

> *Your parents play a big role in your life and they play a big role in your education, because a lot of people who don't have parents or have bad parents don't really care about school.*

In addition to his parents, Ricky says that his older sister has played an important role in his success as a student, especially when he was just starting out and getting accustomed to speaking and learning in English. A second-grader by the time Ricky started kindergarten, his sister "shared some of the things she knew," thus giving Ricky a leg up that helped him succeed despite the initial challenge of learning in a new language. Ricky says his sister also helps him now with subjects such as algebra, which he has already taken even though he is only in seventh grade.

RICKY AT SCHOOL

Since Ricky immigrated before kindergarten, he has no point of refer-
ence against which to evaluate his early schooling experiences in the
United States. In one sense, Ricky did not start school at any disadvan-
tage in comparison to his U.S.-born peers, since he began at age five with
what would generally be considered his age cohort. Moreover, Ricky did
not report any of the kind of personally demoralizing experiences that
other Mexican-born students in the sample talked about with regard
to their earliest teachers in the U.S. (see, in particular, Diana's profile).
Ricky does share, however, that it took him several years to catch up
to some of his peers because most of his early elementary teachers did
not allow the use of Spanish in the classroom: "If you talked Spanish
in school, they got you in trouble." Like Diana, Ricky had one teacher
in his early schooling who was an exception. This teacher, he says,
"started teaching me English a little, translated things for me, and that
helped a lot." Ricky says he also had the opportunity to collaborate in
Spanish with friends and that working in two languages helped him
a great deal initially: "Everything was, like, new to me. I didn't speak
English, and I had never been to school before that. . . . I had some
friends that [also] came from Mexico, so we learned together."

   Now at CCS, Ricky's academic performance provides no hint of any
early struggles. He is viewed both by teachers and his peers as a student leader, and if anything he is far ahead of many of his peers, most
of whom are U.S.-born, in both his current school performance and
his thinking and planning for future academic and vocational pursuits.
Since CCS has an extended school day (students are required to be in
class until 5:00 p.m. on most days), most students there report receiving
little homework. When I ask Ricky about this, however, he points out
that the fact that teachers do not assign homework does not mean he
does not spend time studying at home:

   Well, here they don't give us homework, but since I want to, like, study
   sometimes I give myself homework to do. I sit at the computer and

study something that I find interesting—I give myself some work to do about that. . . . And then with the [state standardized test] coming up, I want to practice algebra. I get some books from the library, and I study and try to do some problems. So I [usually] spend about two hours.

Ricky's grades are exceptional across the board, but he is particularly focused on success in his math and science courses, given his future goal of a career in biochemistry. His standardized test scores reflect this emphasis, and he has received several perfect scores on recent math exams. In addition to math and science, Ricky says he particularly enjoys playing soccer and "doing art," which is strongly emphasized at CCS and provides him with a focused but relaxing break from his work in the courses that are his primary academic priority.

All this is not to say, however, that Ricky does not sometimes slip and fail to meet expectations (mostly his own) and that he does not succumb on occasion to the usual social temptations of a middle school classroom. His notion of an academic slip, however, is telling: "Right now in math class, sometimes I talk a lot and not really work hard, and it's really lowering my grade . . . well, not like a full grade, but a few points."

A STRONG SENSE OF PERSONAL IDENTITY

Although Ricky has clearly benefited from positive and supportive relationships with his parents, siblings, and teachers, he views himself as very much his own person. For example, when he tells me that other students made fun of him in younger grades for being academically inclined, he adds, "I don't care what people say about me." Similarly, when I ask him if he has any role models, Ricky simply replies, "I don't concentrate on other people; I concentrate on myself."

As I did in most interviews, I give Ricky a series of adjectives and ask him to choose which ones he thinks apply to himself. Although somewhat modest, Ricky chooses "smart" and "hard-working." When I ask him to think about whether he believes luck has also played any role in his academic success, his reply reflects the same drive and self-determination he exhibits at other points in the interview:

> *Sometimes luck can help you out a little, but it mostly depends on you. It depends on your determination and your expectations for yourself.*

Then, when asked a brief follow-up question, Ricky immediately brings the conversation back to the people he sees as primarily responsible for his success:

Where do you think you get your determination from?
(Without hesitation.) *My parents.*

LISTENING TO RICKY

Ricky possesses ambition and maturity well beyond his years. In addition to already being savvy about the college application process, having a clear idea of colleges to which he would like to apply and the field he would like to study (which are, of course, subject to change), and having straight A's in his classes, Ricky seems to live a well-balanced student life. He makes time for his friends and enjoys art and soccer as much as math and science, even as he "gives himself homework"—sometimes up to two hours per night—to study "something that [he] finds interesting" to compensate for the fact that students receive little or no homework at CCS.

Even at the young age of twelve, Ricky's sense of independence is evident in response to my question about his having a role model: "I don't concentrate on other people; I concentrate on myself." He also expresses a belief that success "depends on your determination and your expectations for yourself," not what other people can do for you. At the same time, he is quick to credit his parents for having been his primary supports as a high achiever. In some ways, Ricky's parents spur him on academically through what some researchers have called the "don't be like me" syndrome found among many immigrant parents.[1] While on the one hand these parents instill some of their own deeply held values such as hard work, family loyalty and respect, and persistence in the face of adversity, they also send a powerful and consistent message to their children that they do not want them to be like them in other respects. Specifically, they do not want their children to struggle financially in the same ways they have had to, and they want their children to work in professions with far better pay and working conditions than exist in the jobs they are forced to endure.

Researchers have noted that the desire for their children to have a "better life" is particularly prevalent among Mexican immigrant parents who come to the United States to work in the agricultural industry.[2] Despite the fact that many immigrants lack the resources or knowledge of English to provide material support to their children in their K–12 schooling and in the pursuit of college, studies have found that Mexican and other Latino immigrant parents (and immigrant parents in general) tend to be optimistic and ambitious about their children's academic futures—indeed, this is often a primary reason they move to the United States in the first place.[3] Moreover, while teachers and administrators— and sometimes non-immigrant parents—often believe that immigrant parents are uninterested in their children's schooling if they participate in conferences and other school events less frequently than other parents, much of the existing research in this field has shown the opposite to be true. While immigrant parents may in fact be intimidated by some school environments because they speak little English or have relatively low levels of formal education themselves—or they may have difficulty attending some school events because they work long hours—they are among the most active parents in any school community in terms of reinforcing the school's messages at home. Many immigrant parents instill in their children deeply held beliefs about the value of education and the need to persevere in the face of obstacles.[4] To this end, immigrant parents are often willing to, as Ricky explains, "do whatever they can" to help their children achieve their academic goals. As researcher Ricardo D. Stanton-Salazar explains in the book *Manufacturing Hope and Despair*, which synthesizes the results of a study in several Southern California high schools and their surrounding communities:

> *Our interviews with Mexican immigrants clearly show that they held both strong educational values and great hopes for their children. The evidence also shows that most parents do attempt to monitor their adolescent children's progress in school—for example, by reading progress reports and talking with their children. Cognizant of their own limitations due to their often scant educational preparation and their marginal position relative to the cultural mainstream, parents found more culturally appropriate ways of remaining true to their values.[5]*

In contrast to his parents' strong influence on his education, however, Ricky also observes that many of his peers are not as fortunate as he is when it comes to parental support. Since both immigrant and non-immigrant students attend CCS, Ricky is likely referring to students from both of these backgrounds when he says, "A lot of people who don't have parents or have bad parents don't really care about school." The wisdom Ricky shares about parental involvement, both in terms of his own successes and the struggles he sees many of his classmates facing, suggests the need for educators to think in broader terms about what parental support of a child's education looks like and where there may be signs that a student's family is truly disengaged. This poses further questions about the ways educators can make school environments more inviting to immigrant parents and take advantage of the support parents are providing for their children's education at home even if they are absent from conferences and other school events for various reasons. Authors Norma Gonzalez, Luis Moll, and Cathy Amanti suggest that educators should learn how to tap the "funds of knowledge" that exist in the families and communities of their students.[6] More specific ideas for the ways schools can reach out to immigrant parents and take advantage of the resources they offer are included in the concluding section, "Living Up to the Promise."

Karla

"I got friends everywhere in the school, plus the teachers and all that."

Expanding Social Networks over Time

FROM HER FIRST PARTICIPATION in the focus groups at age eighteen, Karla struck me as a young woman who had little difficulty being comfortable in social situations. While certainly not dominating these conversations, it was clear that Karla felt free expressing her opinions about everything from teachers' attitudes about immigrant students (she found some exceedingly helpful and others patronizing and impatient) to the difficulty of portfolio presentations, which are a central part of the assessment practices at NYGHS. It was also apparent that Karla was exceedingly well liked among her peers, and in our individual interview—in which she projected a mature yet friendly air—she confirms that she believes she has made friends easily since coming to NYGHS from Honduras two and a half years earlier:

I don't know, like I'm very friendly with people. Yes, it doesn't take me long [to make friends]. Like, months after I came, like, a lot of people knew me. I was surprised, like, wow—they knew me. When I was in school in Honduras I knew, like, a little bit of people, but when I came here the whole school knew me. Like, yes, I have like a lot of friends right now. Like some of the ninth-graders, they're new in school. . . . I got friends everywhere in the school, plus the teachers and all that.

Although the language barrier at first posed a formidable challenge in Karla's strange new environment—since she knew no English when she arrived—she attributes her wide friendship network both to her own friendliness and to the fact that peers and family members have helped her acclimate quickly. Initially, Karla says that connecting with other Hondurans was key to her gradually building her peer network outward to include students from other cultures:

I remember that when I came the first day the teacher was talking to the students, and I was there, like, "I don't know what they're saying." And I asked some Dominicans, and they speak Spanish, but there are some things in their Spanish that's different, so I was kind of confused, too, and I was frustrated and stuff. Then they put me in one class where there were other Hondurians,[1] and they helped me a lot. They helped me with my homework and all that. And then when I was home, my sister and my cousin, they always was trying to get me to speak English. I was speaking Spanish and they said, "I don't understand." They always tried to get me to speak English, my sister and my cousin. . . .

There were some other Hondurians here, but they were like seniors and stuff, so they were graduating that year. But, yeah, every time that we'd go to lunch after three [morning] classes, I remember if I had homework in those classes they told me to go downstairs [to the cafeteria] with my book bag, and they would translate for me, and they was helping me to do my homework and stuff, and after we was done we would play outside and stuff. They helped me a lot.

I ask Karla if it is typical for students at NYGHS to cluster in friendship groups by cultural origin. While she says that the ability to connect with other Hondurans was critical to her success at the beginning, she adds that both for her and her peers, peer networks cross cultural boundaries regularly at NYGHS once students become comfortable in the social environment:

> *At the beginning, when the school starts, I'd say all Dominicans, all Africans, all Hondurians, they sit by groups. But then like in two months or three months you see everybody—you can see a whole table with only Africans and one Dominican there, and that's how it starts mixing. Then the next week, you see a table with all Africans and three Dominicans . . . we be changing, like, everything around.*
>
> *There were some new boys, like, they're Africans and, like, they're tall. And when they came they would always be, like, with the Africans, and now they don't be with Africans. They always be with the Hondurians and the Mexicans playing soccer. And like, you know how they change. Like, it didn't take them like two weeks. The first week they were, like, quiet, always like that. And now, they're like, "You want to play soccer?" Everybody plays soccer, basketball, they're all together. And even when they play soccer, sometimes there are Dominicans and Africans, but they don't do the teams like that. They don't be like, the Dominicans on one team and the Africans [on the other], so they mix. So I like my school.*

Now that Karla is a senior and has been at NYGHS for more than two years, the tables have turned and she and her peers find themselves in the position of helping younger Honduran students, and other Spanish-speaking students, feel comfortable in their new environment. One of the things that she says makes this kind of student mentoring possible is that classes are clustered in two multiyear groups, with ninth- and tenth-graders taking the same classes and eleventh- and twelfth-graders taking more advanced classes:

We help the ones that doesn't know, like, a lot [of English] and stuff like that. . . . Now, like, if you go to ninth grade or tenth grade, like, nine and ten are in the same classroom. And then, like, yeah, the tenth-graders, like, if a ninth-grader doesn't know what something means, they go and help them. And when I came here the first year, they was helping me; next year I was helping everybody. . . . That makes people's self-esteem go up, too.

SUCCEEDING DESPITE FAMILY SEPARATION

Karla has been separated from both her parents (as well as her younger brother) since she came to the United States. Five years earlier, Karla's mother, a teacher, and her father, a children's soccer coach and retired professional soccer player, sent Karla's sister to live in New York with her aunt and cousins because they believed she could receive a better education in the U.S. than would be available to her in Honduras. Karla's sister had difficulty adjusting to the transition at first, so it made Karla apprehensive when she learned that her parents also planned for her to come to the U.S. for her studies:

My mom, my dad, my other sister, and my little brother, they're still in Honduras. My mom is a high school global [history] teacher, and my dad used to play soccer but now he's retired and now he has a soccer academy for little kids. . . .

My mom knew that I always wanted to be, like, a doctor, and she was trying to, she told me and my sister we could have a better education here. Like the education in Honduras is not bad, but she knew that we would have, like, more opportunities here and success and stuff.

Do you think that's true?
Yeah. (Laughs.) Yeah. . . .

How was it to be separated from your mother and other people in your family?

That was bad, 'cause I remember when my sister came she used to always call Honduras and tell my mom to take her back, that she didn't want to be here, and she was, like, frustrated, and so I was like, "Oh, poor my sister." But then like four years later they told me that I was gonna come here. I was mad, too. I was like, "Oh, the same thing's gonna happen to me!" But, like, I really miss it because I was the only one, like, taking care of my—when my dad and mom was working I was the one taking care of my little sister and my brother—so I really miss them. When they call they always tell me to go back, so I get emotional and stuff.

Karla now lives with her aunt (who has lived in the U.S. for nineteen years), her older sister, and her cousins in a New York City public housing complex. In general, Karla feels safe living in what she refers to as "the projects," even though she has heard about crimes taking place in the surrounding neighborhood, because she is relatively quiet and is uninvolved in street gangs or other issues related to local crime. Being what she calls a "black Honduran," Karla also believes she doesn't draw much attention to herself among the African Americans who live in the complex. She has a reasonably good relationship with her aunt, who primarily speaks Spanish, but she says this relationship has been strained recently because Karla and her sister have higher grades than their cousins who were born in the U.S., a fact that Karla believes makes her aunt jealous:

When the grades come, they [my cousins] are always, like, failing this class or that class, and when mine come it's, like, different. So right now I feel like there's like something with my aunt. I don't know if it's like jealousy or something like that, but she has started, like, treating my sister and me differently than her kids. Because before she used to come to pick up my grades and stuff like that, but now, like, the grades go home or whatever and she doesn't even see them. She doesn't see them because she knows that they're good, and her kids are doing really bad. And she knows that my grades are good, but she doesn't say, "Oh, congratulations!" or something like that. But I don't mind. I know that it's for me; it's not for her.

It is hard to tell if Karla truly does not mind that her aunt has shown less interest in her schoolwork lately or if she is more disappointed than she lets on about the seeming indifference of this primary caregiver in her life. Karla tells me she is excited, however, because her parents, younger sister, and younger brother will all be visiting from Honduras for her high school graduation in a few months, the first time she will have seen them in almost three years.

SCHOOL-BASED FACTORS IN KARLA'S SUCCESS

Despite any deficits that may exist in the adult support Karla is getting at home, she is a highly successful student with an 86 grade-point average. She has passed all the required state Regents exams to graduate and plans to take the trigonometry and chemistry Regents to get an advanced diploma. She is passing all her classes with A's and B's, even though she still finds portfolio assessment difficult (which she discussed in the focus group sessions several months earlier), and she says that her current math class is "killing me" because she feels the teacher's expectations are unclear. After graduation, Karla plans to study nursing at the same community college that her sister currently attends, then transfer to a four-year college for pre-med studies and ultimately become a pediatrician.

One of the primary factors that has made Karla feel more confident as a student over the last two and a half years is that she feels her command of English has vastly improved. She knows this, she says, because she no longer mentally translates instructions or ideas into Spanish but finds that she is now able to "think in English":

Now I feel like, I feel comfortable. Like they [teachers] speak in English and stuff like that and I understand. And something that I realized is that when they used to speak English to me before, I would translate

everything in Spanish in my mind. And now sometimes in class now, like,
I'm proud of myself, 'cause I don't need to translate.

In addition, Karla marks her progress in English by her performance on the global history Regents exam. She missed a passing grade by four points on her first attempt but passed on her second try—when she did not request a Spanish translation:

I didn't pass the global [history Regents exam], because in global we
have to do the DBQ [document-based question, which requires students
to answer questions based on historical documents]. And these are like
a lot—I didn't understand that a lot. And the first time I took it I had
a copy in Spanish, and I thought that would be easier. And I didn't pass
that, I had like 61, and then next time I did it only in English and I
passed it. So I was like, "Wow—that's really funny!"

Karla says teachers have played a key role both in her acquisition of English and in her academic success overall. In addition to connecting Karla with other Honduran students, as well Spanish-speaking students from other countries, Karla had a biology teacher in ninth and tenth grade who translated lessons for her and taught her some of the basics of English grammar:

I remember Ms. Elizabeth, she knew a little bit of Spanish. So when I
came, like, she was trying to translate some things for me to just speak
to me. Like, she used to say the things in English first for the other stu-
dents and then she used to translate them for me in Spanish. And then
she told me, like . . . [she] taught me about words in the past and the
future and all that.

More recently, Karla says two other teachers have played a significant role in her success during her junior and senior years. She credits her English literature teacher, Ms. Sheila, with pushing her and her peers beyond a level that even they believed they could achieve. At first, Karla says she and her classmates were resistant to Ms. Sheila's insistence on high-level work, but she has since realized (even if not all of her peers have done so) that Ms. Sheila's high expectations are just what she needs in order to be ready for college:

> *Ms. Sheila, my English teacher, even though we act like we don't like her, all the pressure that she puts on us, like, she give us books and then she be like, "Oh, read from chapter 1 to 10 like two days later," and then she'd give us like—even though we be like, "No!" That was good because we're gonna have to do more than that in college. And the essays, she want everything perfect, like, the grammar, everything is like—she help me a lot, like, with words. And, like, now me and my friends, last year we were so frustrated with her, because we came from eleventh grade . . . and now we can write essays like fifteen pages, ten pages, so she helped us a lot.*
>
> *She put a lot of pressure on us and she knows what she's doing, and she knows what she has to do—when she needs to be rude with us, when she needs to be, like, on us. She knows how to work with us. She's the only one who can, like, really control us. She was pregnant and she left for months, and we was like not doing nothing. The other teachers, like, they don't give us homework like that, so we was like, we were not doing anything in school. And then she came back, you see everybody do homework. Even on Facebook now, [students say] like, "I gotta do Ms. Sheila's homework!" She encourages us to do all our jobs.*

The other teacher that Karla says plays a significant role in her success is Ms. Audrey, her U.S. history teacher, who is also helping her navigate the college application process. In addition to providing her with advice and assistance in school, Ms. Audrey nominated Karla for a four-day program that teaches students about applying to college, which took place on a suburban campus nearby:

> *Ms. Audrey right now, the U.S. [history] teacher, like, she knows history and stuff, and, like, she's helping me a lot to get scholarships and all that. She helps me with the applications to the scholarships and stuff like*

that. And she also sent me to the program Pathway to College—like, over there we write our personal statements, they explain everything about college, how to apply, loans, grants. We went there for four days, and like they teach you, like, almost everything that we need to do, to be careful in school and other stuff. So that helped me a lot.

Karla says it was difficult when she and her classmates first arrived at Pathway to College because they were the only immigrant students among seven schools attending the program. But she adds that this concern dissipated quickly, quite possibly due to her and her classmates' ability to make friends easily:

They put all the schools together [in the dormitories]. . . . We were the only global school, so we were a little bit nervous since, like, those kids talk English, like, perfect. . . . But then they [the other students] started asking us questions. . . . After the first day, we were the ones that were talking the most.

Karla's plan is to enroll in the community college that her older sister attends to study nursing, then transfer after two years as a pre-med to one of the state university campuses that has a well-known medical school. Her ultimate goal is to become a pediatrician, an ambition that she says stems from her caregiving role to her younger siblings and cousins, whom she left behind in Honduras:

How did you decide you wanted to be a pediatrician?
I used to take care of my other sister and my two cousins, so I don't know—I just like kids, and I don't know. One time that my mom, she went to work, and we were there by ourselves. We went outside, and we were not supposed to go outside. And my sister was playing with her bicycle and she fell, and she hurt herself in her knee, and—I don't know, something came at me. And it said, like, "You know, you know how to, like, fix what happened and, like, you should do it." So I took her—we were the same height—and I took her on my back and I put her on the couch, and I told my other two cousins to come in the house. First, I put some water and then I put alcohol and then I put

a bandage there. I thought, "My mom's gonna do something to us when she came [home]." But she just told me that she was really proud of me, because I knew how to take care of the situation, even though I wasn't the oldest one. And that stayed on my mind and my heart—I don't know. And since then I'm always helping people.

Even though Karla says she likes living in the United States and feels as though it affords her a lot of valuable opportunities, she also says, "I always remember my roots. I know where I came from." She thus already has a plan for her life after medical school that involves practicing medicine in both countries as well as elsewhere:

I really want to stay here, like, to be a pediatrician. I want to stay here, like, maybe three years and then I want to go to Honduras and give them, like, all the help that I can. Since I was little, I really wanted to go to Africa, so I'm planning to go there. I'm going to work there. Yeah, I think I'm going to go to Africa.

A SENSE OF RESPONSIBILITY TO OTHERS

Like several of the other immigrant youth profiled in this book, Karla's ties both to her family and her country of origin are tinged with a sense of responsibility and the desire to help the people she left behind live a better life. When I ask Karla why she thinks she is successful, she brings the conversation back to her family, and her words sound like those of several other students I interviewed who have a desire to "give back" for the many sacrifices their families have made:

Why do you think you are successful?
Because I'm responsible, I think, and because I know what I want. I know why I am in this country. And I don't know—like, I want to help my mom and my dad. Like, they was always, even though they had problems and stuff they was always trying to give the best to us. . . . We try and, like, do our best to give them the same thing that our parents gave us in our childhood. So we want to do the same thing for them.

Even as a high school student, Karla feels a sense of responsibility to some of her peers who are not experiencing the same level of success that she is. Karla seems to view relationships and academic success as linked both for her and her friends, and she feels an obligation to help her friends bring up their grades even if it means sacrificing some activities she loves:

> *I help my partners right now. If they need help, I tell them to call me. Right now my best friend, they didn't put us in the same class. I don't know why, because we've been together since the beginning and, like, they [had] put us together [before] and everything was stronger. Now, like, I went down a little bit [academically] and she went down a lot. I try to help her a lot, and now she has to present [her] portfolio and, like, she's like very frustrated. So . . . sometimes if I have like—if she needs my help I prefer to miss my soccer practice. . . . She's missing, like, one Regents, two Regents, and I really want to graduate with her.*

When I ask Karla to offer her advice to teachers on helping all immigrant students succeed in school, including those like her friend who are struggling, she repeats a word used by almost everyone who was interviewed for this project—*patience*—even as she recognizes that teachers can face some significant challenges working with students who have recently arrived in the U.S.:

> *I would say to have patience. And, like, I know that at first they're [immigrant students are] frustrated, and sometimes they can be rude and stuff like that. But still to have patience and try to give the best to help them. Yeah, I think patience, because the first time [teachers meet immigrant students], you're going to see a lot of things from those kids.*

LISTENING TO KARLA

In terms of the various types of engagement that support immigrant students' success, as discussed earlier in this book, Karla is clearly an example of a student whose relational engagement has played a central role in her success at school since she came to the United States.[2] From her first days two and a half years ago as a new student at NYGHS who knew virtually no English, Karla has succeeded both academically and socially by gradually expanding her social network, beginning with a handful of other Honduran and Spanish-speaking students in her classes, to a larger network of Honduran peers at NYGHS, and, ultimately, to classmates representing a variety of cultures and languages of origin. While Karla's natural gregariousness is clearly a factor in her ability to make friends easily, language has also played a key role in her ability to connect with peers at all stages in her development as a student. Finding Honduran peers who not only spoke Spanish but spoke it in a way she could understand (a connection that was facilitated by teachers) was key to connecting Karla with Honduran students in the school from other grades. As the older Honduran students helped Karla with her homework, she became more confident both as a student and as a speaker of English, which allowed her to expand her friendships beyond Spanish-speaking students to those with whom she shares common interests. Now, as a senior, Karla works with new Spanish-speaking students to help them acclimate to the school and language, in a sense completing the circle of relational engagement that began upon her arrival.

As discussed by Omar in his portrait, Karla perceives a sense of cross-cultural community at NYGHS that makes it possible for her to engage with diverse peers across cultural and age barriers. She observes this same kind of interaction taking place among her classmates—for example, students newly arrived from various cultures playing basketball and soccer together (and not dividing the teams by country), and the gradual mixing of cafeteria tables to include students with different languages of origin. Karla seems to recognize that this sense of community might not exist in all high schools, and she ends her description of the many diverse friendships she sees forming around her by saying, "I like my school."

Karla's satisfaction with NYGHS also seems to be related to her relationships with several teachers: Ms. Elizabeth, who helped her when she first arrived by translating biology lessons into English and helping her learn verb conjugations; Ms. Audrey, who has helped her navigate the college application process and find financial aid opportunities, and who nominated her for a college information summit outside of school; and Ms. Sheila, who holds Karla and her classmates to extremely high academic standards, which Karla recognizes are helping them build skills that will be essential for future success in college. Although Karla says that she and her classmates often "act like we don't like [Ms. Sheila], the pressure she puts on us," Karla seems to have a deep appreciation for the belief that Ms. Sheila shows in her ability to complete high-level work. This is in contrast to other teachers mentioned by Karla, Omar, and other students in this study who, as the students perceive it, send messages that communicate relatively low opinions of their immigrant students' skills and abilities.

Although Karla enjoys positive engagement on many levels at school, her home and family situation has been the source of stress in her life. Karla's separation from her parents and younger siblings, whom she has not seen for two and a half years, represents a situation that is common among immigrant families, whereby children are sent to the United States with the hope of better educational opportunities even if other family members are not able to immigrate with them.[3] As Karla describes, this separation from parents and other immediate family members is often a source of considerable emotional distress.[4] She discusses her feelings of longing when her family calls from Honduras, especially when her younger siblings ask her to go back: "I get emotional and stuff." Karla does not seem to pay a significant academic price for the distress this causes her, even though there is tension with her aunt, her primary caregiver in the U.S., over what Karla perceives as jealousy about her high achievement. Yet it is clear that Karla does not feel as emotionally supported by her aunt as she would feel if her parents were in the United States, and she is eagerly looking forward to her parents' arrival for her graduation from NYGHS.

As Karla looks ahead, it is striking that she is one of three young women interviewed for this project whose ambition is to become a pediatrician. In Karla's voice, we hear a sense of commitment to others and—as other students expressed in their interviews—an emotional connection to the country she left behind and a desire to "give them all the help I can." We hear this same sense of service in Karla's relationship with some of her classmates at NYGHS—the younger students she helps because they are just learning English and the friend she is helping to pass the Regents exams so that they can graduate together. Karla is one of numerous students interviewed for this study who views her academic skill as not just something that will benefit her in the future but also something that she has a responsibility to apply in service to others.

Ibrahim

~

"My parents have already told me . . .
I'm losing my roots."

The Sacrifices of
Becoming American

SEVENTEEN-YEAR-OLD IBRAHIM is that student you might meet in virtually any high school, the one who seems to know everyone in the building. Gregarious and almost always smiling, I have seen Ibrahim numerous times at NYGHS since our interview, passing between classes, helping out in the main office, or watching international soccer matches with his friends on television during lunch. He never fails to give me an enthusiastic hello and to ask me how the book is going and when it is coming out. Although Ibrahim is by no means a straight-A student, his grades are solid enough for him to be admitted to some colleges, and several teachers mention his name when I ask them who they believe are the "successful students" at the school. Ibrahim thus exudes an air of competence despite his merely passable grades, and while he is currently not as career-focused as some of his peers, he seems poised for future success by virtue of the fact that he is bright, thoughtful, and immediately likable. As is the case for many high school students, the main obstacle that keeps Ibrahim from achieving higher grades than he currently does is simply, as he puts it, "I'm not organized."

When I ask Ibrahim how he spends his time outside of school, his answer sounds like one that any typical American teenager might offer: "[I'm] with my friends, or I'm just on the computer, on the phone, texting . . . Facebook . . ." Deeply steeped in American popular culture, one of Ibrahim's idols is the rapper Lil Wayne, and his future ambition is to be "either an FBI agent or a soccer player."

Based on Ibrahim's interests, I am not surprised at first by his answer to my question, "Do you consider yourself more American or African?" His response, however, also signals a longing, at least on some level, for the life he left behind:

I would say American, because my parents already told me that. Even my parents already told me that I'm losing my roots, I'm losing my roots.

Are they upset about it?
Of course they should be upset about it.

As was surprisingly common among the students in the NYGHS group, Ibrahim is able to name quickly the exact date that he moved to the United States: September 11. (Of course, the historical significance of the date obviously makes it difficult for him to forget.) Ibrahim and his family came to the U.S. from Togo in West Africa two years and nine months before he was interviewed. When he arrived, Ibrahim spoke French and knew several Togolese languages, but he says he came to the U.S. knowing virtually no English. He describes his early days at NYGHS as "terrible" as he struggled with a new language and completely different expectations than he had grown accustomed to in Togo. During his first few months in the U.S., Ibrahim recalls having been so homesick that, "When I first came, I was calling [Togo] every day—every minute, I was calling."

For one thing, having grown up Muslim, Ibrahim was unaccustomed to the physical closeness of opposite sexes that he encountered at NYGHS. In talking about how expectations were different in his new environment, Ibrahim says:

> *I would say [things are different] not just in the school, but the whole country. According to my religion, women and boys, we're supposed to be separate. We're not supposed to, even like in the class, we're supposed to be far away from each other. Also, like, give a hug—no, we don't do that in my religion. You see somebody, you just say a few words, which is a greeting. You say* salaam alaikum. *That's it.*[1]

When I follow up by asking Ibrahim how he feels about physical proximity to girls now that he has been in the U.S. for a while, he simply answers, "I don't mind."

In terms of other differences in schooling to which Ibrahim needed to adjust, he reiterates and expands on some of what he shared in the focus groups. Specifically, Ibrahim had been one of several vocal participants in the group interviews when the issue of corporal punishment came up, revealing that in schools in some West African countries, students are "whipped" if they do not meet teachers' academic or behavioral expectations: "School in Togo, they put pressure on the student, not verbally but physically. And also a lot of difference. You get whipped for not doing homework, for being late." Although Ibrahim finds his school in the U.S. generally more difficult than those he left behind in Togo, primarily because of the need to do all his work in English, he believes some teachers at NYGHS allow students to get away with too much.

Ibrahim had high hopes for life in the United States when his family first made the decision to immigrate. According to Ibrahim, his parents were motivated primarily by the promise of "opportunity" and a desire to provide a better education for him and his siblings. He adds, however, that he has realized after having lived in New York for nearly three years that it is not the "utopia" (his word) he had originally imagined it to be. Echoing some of the sentiments expressed by Omar in his portrait, Ibrahim still views the United States as a place of plentiful opportunity, but he also has a somewhat negative impression of life in the U.S. because he doesn't view it as a safe place to live: "In my personal point of view, I just don't think the United States is a safe place. The United States is like the number-one country, but it's not safe, it's not safe." When I ask him if he has had personal experiences that have led him to view his environment as unsafe, the usually ebullient Ibrahim becomes sober and pensive as he reveals both his own encounters with street violence and an incident that led to the death of one of his friends:

> *Yeah, I got jumped about two weeks ago.* (Pauses.) *Two boys jumped me—yeah.*

> **Did they take anything from you?**
> *Yeah. I just think United States is not a safe place.*

> **Had anything like that ever happened to you before?**
> *To my friends, yeah. A lot of my friends. They even killed one of my friends.*

Ibrahim is referring here to the killing of an NYGHS senior that stunned the school community a year before our interview. The student, who was to be part of NYGHS's first graduating class several weeks later, was stabbed to death on the street after a group of youth followed him out of a McDonald's.

In addition to the fact that he is African, Ibrahim also believes he is something of a target on the street (though not at NYGHS) because he is Muslim. Ibrahim's father is deeply religious and requires Ibrahim to attend mosque on Saturdays and Sundays, and sometimes also after school. He relates an incident in which he wore white for a religious holiday and was taunted by other youths in the neighborhood, and another encounter that contributed to his feeling unsafe wearing African-style clothes around the city. My question about whether he has ever experienced discrimination since living in the United States leads to the following exchange:

Have you ever been discriminated against here?
Yeah, based on the religion.

Can you talk about that a little bit?
Actually, I remember it was our holiday, so we are supposed to wear white. I just wore white. I was walking outside and they started calling me Osama bin Laden. . . .

Kids from this school?
Not from this school. And also I don't feel comfortable wearing my African dress. . . . It made me sad. I remember [once], I get in an elevator. It was all Americans, and the elevator was not moving. Here goes some guy, "This elevator is only for Americans. The African guy [had] better get out."

Although Ibrahim is now accustomed to Western life and doubts that he will ever move back to Togo to live (though he was planning to return for a visit the summer following our interview), he still has concerns about his safety and for this reason believes he might settle "somewhere in the Euro" after he completes his education. In the following exchange, his voice also seems tinged with some regret, or at least ambivalence, about the fact that becoming more westernized means leaving an important part of himself behind:

I'm forgetting everything from my culture.

You think you're forgetting—
A lot.

Like, what kinds of things?
Everything.

How does it make you feel?
(Pauses.) *I can't say nothing about it. Like, it just happened—* (Pauses.)

It just is what it is?
(Quietly.) *Yeah.*

EXPERIENCES AND RELATIONSHIPS THAT FOSTER IBRAHIM'S SUCCESS

Ibrahim began NYGHS as a ninth-grader and says that things began to pick up for him academically and socially around tenth grade, when his English had greatly improved and he gained considerably more confidence. In addition to television (particularly cartoons), rap music, and other media that he consumed readily as a new American teenager, Ibrahim credits several experiences for a turnaround in his attitude, comfort level, and ability to succeed academically as he entered tenth grade.

Ibrahim particularly cites a supplemental summer and afterschool program run by the Newcomer Youth Resource Alliance (NYRA) as having made a tremendous difference in his ability to succeed at school and to feel comfortable as an American teenager. NYRA is a program that helps ease the transition of immigrants from various countries and provides supplemental services to immigrant children and youth through connections with schools. For Ibrahim, the NYRA program's focus on both academic and nonacademic support helped him feel comfortable using English in a variety of social and academic settings and improved his confidence greatly as he entered tenth grade (as evidenced by his repetition of the phrase "a lot" in the following statement):

> [NYRA] helped me a lot—a lot . . . with homework. I took summer school over there, we took classes—drama, math class—it helped me a lot . . . with English—a lot.

Ibrahim believes that upon entering tenth grade, with the help of NYRA programs he was able to feel comfortable learning in English in a way he had not before. Now, he sees English as absolutely essential to his success in the United States and becomes animated when I ask him how important he thinks it is:

> You really need to speak English to succeed. English is like the number-one language. You want to speak it. So it's real important.

Ibrahim says he has mostly French-speaking friends at school, and they sometimes speak French (or a combination of French and English) in social situations. Ibrahim also has a somewhat multicultural friendship circle, though, and he therefore develops his English skills further with other, non–French-speaking friends, since it is their only common language:

My friends, we always speak in French . . . or mix it—mix English with French.

Do you have other friends who don't speak French?
Oh, yeah!

So with them what do you do?
English. A few of my friends don't speak French. I think it's better, too. I think it's good, because when I'm speaking with them, that's practicing English.

As many other students in the *Portraits of Promise* study did, Ibrahim cites one special teacher as having been a consistent source of support for him ever since ninth grade. When Ibrahim first came to the U.S., he entered Ms. Lori's class after the school year had already begun, feeling lost. Because of the school's looping system for ninth and tenth grades, he had Ms. Lori again for English in his sophomore year and was able to continue developing what he was beginning to experience as a very supportive relationship. Now that he is in his senior year, Ibrahim has not been in Ms. Lori's class for nearly two years, but he still says this relationship has been the single most important factor in his ability to keep meeting the challenges of NYGHS as he prepares for graduation:

Ms. Lori, any time, any kind of problem I have, I always go to her. I know she'll help me. Ms. Lori, she helped me a lot. I don't know how to thank her back. She helped me a lot, from ninth grade to twelfth. She is not my teacher anymore, but any time I need something, I go to her for anything. . . . We [Ms. Lori and I] have a lot of trust.

In the focus groups at NYGHS, several students complained that they believed some of their teachers were racist, or at least held negative attitudes about immigrant students (that they were not as smart as U.S.-born students, that they were difficult to understand, etc.). I ask Ibrahim if he believes his teachers are racist, and his response does not necessarily reflect this notion but instead a more general sense of favoritism among NYGHS educators: "Many teachers, they don't really discriminate, but they know who they like."

In addition to his relationship with Ms. Lori, Ibrahim perceives that there is a multilevel support system at work at NYGHS and at home to help him achieve his goals. Since Ibrahim believes he is "not really good at math," his sister helps him a fair amount with his mathematics homework. Ibrahim also has a cousin who has been in the United States since he was five (the cousin is now eighteen). This cousin has become a kind of mentor to Ibrahim in recent years, helping him learn English and navigate many of the complexities of American life. Moreover, in contrast to many students who resent state standardized tests, Ibrahim believes that the "whole state" is helping him prepare for his future by requiring him to pass the Regents exams to graduate. (He still had two tests to complete for graduation at the time of our interview.) "Actually not just NYRA, but like the whole state, like the Regents, like writing essays prepares you for college."

Ibrahim expresses optimism when I ask him what he envisions for his future: "I see myself good—yeah, that's what I think." He adds that he believes he can achieve any goal as long as he does not experience significant setbacks in his personal life that might distract him from a focus on school. Now that he has survived the initial traumas of immigration, homesickness, and having to learn in a completely new environment and language, Ibrahim believes his personal attitude of happiness is his most important asset:

You know, when you feel happy, like, when your life, when everything's good, you do everything right. You can't work when you're not feeling happy—you're going to be thinking about something.

When I ask Ibrahim to tell me about a topic or project in school about which he is particularly enthusiastic, he chooses his recent reading of Paulo Coelho's novel *The Alchemist*, in which the protagonist travels through Africa to fulfill his personal destiny. Ibrahim's description of the novel's themes of fate and interdependence seems a metaphor for his own journey as an immigrant student from Africa, a journey that has presented him with considerable challenges but that he is also navigating successfully with the help of key mentors and other significant people in his life:

> *I just finished* [The Alchemist] *about three weeks ago. That book is very important. I think everybody should read it.*
>
> **What did you like about it?**
> *[It's] about, like, when something is real and there is no way, like nothing can change it, it must happen. And when you need help, people are here to help you.*

LISTENING TO IBRAHIM

My interview with Ibrahim revealed that, beneath his smile, friendliness, and optimistic outlook on school and his future—all of which I believe are genuine—lies a complex set of feelings related in one way or another to his experiences as an immigrant student. Perhaps the most striking aspect of Ibrahim's story is the extent to which he does not feel safe in New York and the experiences that have led him to this assessment of his current environment. In addition to having been "jumped" several times on the street, Ibrahim is obviously deeply saddened by the death of his friend in an act of violence. Although the murder of Ibrahim's friend did not take place in the neighborhood immediately surrounding the school, the school's immediate vicinity has been subject to waves of theft and other street crime, leading school officials at times to direct students to avoid certain blocks. All these experiences speak to the fact that a large proportion of immigrants in U.S. cities live in neighborhoods with high concentrations of poverty, and that an immigrant child in an urban area is more likely than a U.S.-born child to attend school in a neighborhood surrounded by drugs, gangs, and other risks to their safety and well-being.[2]

Specifically, Ibrahim's account, like those of other NYGHS students, points to conflicts that can exist between immigrant youth and U.S.-born youth in these neighborhoods. Ibrahim feels especially targeted on the street as a Muslim, having been subject to slurs suggesting that he is a terrorist—a particular problem facing Muslim youth since September 11, 2001—and he therefore does not feel safe wearing African or Muslim garb in public.[3] Although Ibrahim says he does not experience such problems in school, he had difficulty in his early days of schooling in the U.S. reconciling certain social conventions he saw around him (such as the close physical proximity between boys and girls) with the teachings of his Muslim upbringing.

Ibrahim's voice is tinged with considerable sadness as he realizes he is forgetting aspects of his culture and, as he puts it, "losing my roots." His story thus highlights the potential importance of what sociologists Alejandro Portes and Rubén Rumbaut have called "selective acculturation," which they define as taking place when children from immigrant families "acculturate to American ways without abandoning their parents' language and key elements of their culture."[4] In addition to mitigating the sense of loss when aspects of language and culture are forgotten, Portes and Rumbaut note that selective acculturation makes it easier for parents to guide their children, support their scholastic achievement, and protect them from risk.[5]

Despite his longing for his native culture and the negative experiences Ibrahim has had since coming to the United States, he seems genuinely engaged both in his schooling and in American culture, and he says again and again that he views English as critical to his chances for a bright future: "You really need to speak English to succeed. English is like the number-one language. You want to speak it. So it's real important." Like other students portrayed in this book, Ibrahim contradicts arguments by anti-immigration advocates that English is at risk as the primary language in the U.S. as more and more immigrants arrive here. As Rumbaut notes in other writing, history has proven that as immigrants come the U.S., "It is the immigrants' mother tongue [not English] that atrophies over time, and quickly."[6] As Ibrahim embodies, the desire to maintain roots with one's country of origin and the desire to learn English and acculturate into American society as effectively as possible are not mutually exclusive.

Finally, Ibrahim's story highlights what other accounts in *Portraits of Promise*, as well as prior research, illustrate: that high-quality relationships with individual teachers, particularly those that last over time, can be a vital resource for immigrant students. As researcher Ricardo Stanton-Salazar has noted, supportive relationships between immigrant students and their teachers or counselors are especially important assets if they are marked by longevity (often continuing past a student's enrollment in a particular teacher's class), confidentiality, and openness to talk about issues beyond academics.[7]

On the other hand, Ibrahim was one of several students who said he finds his teachers at NYGHS to be too lax about student discipline. Ibrahim's comments in this vein are especially noteworthy in light of Karla's in the last chapter, in which she suggests that most of her teachers (except for Ms. Sheila) do not push their students hard enough to do high-level work. While obviously not providing a sufficient argument in favor of corporal punishment at NYGHS or elsewhere, these students' viewpoints raise important questions about the level of motivation and discipline that immigrant students, especially those who are successful, might be looking for from their teachers. The implications of these questions are discussed in more detail in the concluding section, "Living Up to the Promise."

Eduardo

"[With some teachers] we just have fun, talk, laugh, and it makes me forget about stuff from home, like problems and stuff like that. And then others just want to talk about the problems and try to help me find solutions to those."

Turning to Teachers as a Sounding Board

EDUARDO IMMIGRATED to the United States with his family from Mexico when he was a year and a half old. A pensive and articulate sixteen-year-old, Eduardo has no recollection of life in Mexico and has only attended school in the United States. By some definitions, this would make him part of the 1.5 generation, young people who "are born abroad but arrive in their new homeland prior to the age of twelve, exposing them to the new country's schools and culture during their formative years."[1] He is in virtually all respects an American teenager, and the problems he discusses in his interview could be those of any of his classmates, whether born in the U.S. or not. In some respects, however, issues that affect Eduardo's life are directly related to his growing up in a Mexican immigrant family, particularly one whose primary source of income has been California's agricultural industry.

Eduardo's parents, both of whom were field-workers when he was small, divorced several years prior to his interview, a situation that seems to cause stress for him now. He recalls that when his parents were still together and were both working, he and his siblings would sometimes accompany one of them to "the fields" if his parents could not find anyone to look after the children:

> They'd have to go to work, but then, like, they couldn't get anyone to take care of me, so I would have to go with them. . . . If we [my siblings and I] weren't asleep or the work wasn't too hard, like, if it was something really simple, they'd put us to do something.

Now Eduardo lives primarily with his mother, older sister, and younger brother, although he also stays with his father and his father's longtime partner every other week. Eduardo gets along well with his father and the woman he refers to as his "stepmom" and has a good time on Sundays when they "usually just have fun and go out and eat." Eduardo says his father is relatively financially stable because he has risen to a supervisory position, and since "his house is actually in the middle of the fields . . . he has work in the winter even when people are getting laid off." Eduardo says he has more difficulty connecting with his mother, who has also risen to a supervisory position, because she works extremely long hours and has a long commute that requires her to travel among three different factories in the region:

> My mom works longer hours [than my father]. Sometimes she'll be there [at home], but sometimes she'll be tired. She's usually always driving and she says she gets really tired, because, I mean, those are long hours. And so usually she'll make some food, make us dinner, then she goes into her room, and I do the same thing. She'll have me translate papers and

things like that that are in English, so that is when we usually talk. And
when I have to ask her for permission to go somewhere or to do some-
thing, that is when we usually talk.

By Eduardo's account, the fact that his mother is overwhelmed by her
work-related responsibilities—combined with the fact that she does not
speak much English—means she is unable to offer him the kind of parental support that other students who attend CCS cite as important to
their success.

Other aspects of Eduardo's family situation that contribute to his
stress are that his sister has struggled with a chronic illness that has
affected her academic performance and his older brother has left home
and maintains little contact with the family. Even though Eduardo is a
middle child, he says there is an extra responsibility on him to be the
"role-model child" and set an example of academic success and positive
behavior for his younger brother:

> *My mom and dad, I want to say that they've pretty much both given me*
> *the title of role-model child. They want my [younger] brother to do, like,*
> *stuff like I'm doing and get good grades and stuff. And they want me to*
> *check up on him and make sure he's going on the right path.*

Eduardo's parents' wish that he be the "role-model child" is height-
ened by the fact that they are immigrants who, as he explains, have
sacrificed a great deal so that their children could have better learning
opportunities in the United States. In describing his parents' motivation
for immigrating, Eduardo says:

> *They wanted us to have better opportunities, even if it meant them working*
> *their entire lives like that, in the fields. They still wanted us to have a better*
> *education and more opportunities than what we would get in Mexico.*

Do you think that's true [that opportunities are better in the
United States]?

It is. Like, over there probably I wouldn't be able to, like, have really gone to college much because of how the economic status is over there. So, it's pretty bad over there, and here it's more stable than it is in Mexico.

Since his mother knows little English, Eduardo says he speaks Spanish about 70 percent of the time at home, and about 80 percent of the time when he is with his father. Eduardo's father knows more English than his mother, but Eduardo says his father insists that his children continue to speak Spanish with him as a way of "keeping in touch with our roots and not losing our heritage." Eduardo's father, for example, insists that the children only speak Spanish when their grandparents are visiting. Eduardo points to a growing tension between him and his siblings on the one hand and his father on the other, however, as a cultural and linguistic divide develops between them: "It gets harder with my dad, because we're more integrated into American society."

THE COMPENSATORY ROLE OF TEACHERS

Because of the long hours Eduardo's mother works and the fact that he only lives with his father occasionally, relationships with teachers are especially important to him. For one thing, Eduardo says of his teachers, "They usually give me the basics of what I need to get into college, and how to get there, like which classes I would take, like, prerequisite classes." At this point in his junior year, Eduardo plans to study architecture, perhaps at UCLA, even though his mother (like Omar's) wants him to become a doctor. Eduardo says he is keeping an open mind and is considering a variety of colleges and fields. A recent career day at CCS piqued his interest in engineering, especially since science and math are his favorite subjects, and students at CCS learn about colleges and the application process in advisory, a class focused on helping students achieve personal and academic goals. Although the choice of a college major can seem overwhelming to a high school junior, Eduardo says his advisory teacher, Mr. Blair, serves as a source of helpful advice by encouraging Eduardo and his classmates to consider the pros and cons of various fields of study before they make a commitment:

> *My advisory teacher, usually he's kind of straight up a little bit, because he would give the bad parts first [about a particular field students might be interested in pursuing] and the good parts later, so it makes us think about it first.*

Eduardo says that Mr. Blair and Ms. Alvarez, the mathematics teacher cited by several other students from CCS, are the most supportive adults in his life now and, along with a few other teachers, mentor him in ways his parents are currently unable to do. In some cases, Eduardo says he and his favorite teachers "just have fun, talk, and laugh," which allows him to "forget about stuff." In other cases, Eduardo draws on the support of these teacher-mentors to unburden himself of some of the pressures he feels as a "role-model child" to his family and to work out solutions to some of the issues that trouble him at home:

> *They [teachers] help me relieve stress from home. Some of the teachers know the problems [at home], and some of them try to, like, talk to me. And others, we just have fun, talk, laugh, and it makes me forget about stuff from home, like problems and stuff like that. And then others just want to talk about the problems and try to help me find solutions to those.*

In addition to the teachers upon whom Eduardo relies, he has a few friends who are important members of his support system. Eduardo says that, in general, "everyone gets along pretty well" at CCS and that students support one another's success. For example, to help him meet the challenges of his English class—which Eduardo considers one of his weaker subjects even though his most recent grade in a CCS English class was an A—Eduardo has a friend who he says is "pretty much in love with literature and writing and stuff—he helps me with the structure of my essays and grammar and all that stuff." In addition, Eduardo's girlfriend is also a high-achieving student, and the two motivate each other to succeed: "My girlfriend, she pushes me a lot to do good in school, and I do the same for her."

SIGHTS SET ON THE FUTURE

Eduardo's strong motivation to succeed, while certainly fueled by the "push" he receives from his teachers and friends, also seems to be driven by his own intellectual curiosity and thirst for learning. Despite the fact that CCS teachers give little or no homework (because school is in session from 8 a.m. to 5 p.m.), Eduardo says he spends about ninety minutes per night doing schoolwork and often "stays up until 2:00 or 3:00 doing research on different topics." When I ask Eduardo what he sees himself doing in ten years, he suggests that he is in no hurry to stop growing intellectually: "I'll probably still be in college." As a junior in high school, Eduardo has so far taken two college-level courses through a special program at his school, and although he has struggled a bit to meet their advanced academic requirements, he remains enthusiastic about this opportunity his school affords him to earn college credit and plans to take more college courses before he graduates from CCS.

In addition to academics, Eduardo is involved in music and several sports, about which he says, "They keep me from doing anything that I'll regret." Eduardo says that at times older youth have tried to introduce him to alcohol and marijuana, but Eduardo says he is determined to avoid these risks and to stay focused on his academic and career goals:

> *My brother . . . he smoked [marijuana] and had friends who were smoking. Some of them would, like, try to get me to go where they were going and stuff. But then I wouldn't go with them. And the same thing with drinking. My brother used to drink. I don't know—I don't think he still does. But he used to. Some of his friends do and some of them were like in gangs or something. And so I guess my brother sort of fell into that, but I would stay away. I wouldn't go with them and wouldn't spend time with any of them.*

Finally, when I ask Eduardo to think about what makes him hopeful as he looks ahead to his future, he returns to the central role that key relationships play in supporting him to be successful:

As you look ahead, what are some things that you have right now that make you optimistic about your future?

The relationships with friends and teachers. Like I know that they would be there for me when I need help and I would do the same for them. And for teachers just, like, I could just talk to them or e-mail and stuff in case I need help, or if I just need or want to talk or something. . . . I have a lot of people pushing me and helping me to go forward, to keep going, and not give up and stuff like that.

LISTENING TO EDUARDO

Like Karla, as profiled in her portrait, Eduardo is a student for whom relational engagement is key to his success at school and seems to make a critical difference in his ability to remain on a positive path. In Eduardo's case, the relationships he has with teachers seem to be the most important aspect of his academic support system in that they serve in a compensatory capacity, providing a kind of support that Eduardo's parents are unable to give him at home. While two other CCS students, Diana and Ricky, both emphasize their parents' motivation as important reasons why they are doing well in school, Eduardo seems to recognize that he lacks the same level of support that some of his peers possess in this regard. The divorce of Eduardo's parents forces him to live in separate homes, and it is clear from his story that he is for the most part a "latchkey teenager," one who needs to live largely independently because of his mother's work schedule.

At the same time, Eduardo does not seem resentful of his home situation. He is well aware of the sacrifices his parents have made to benefit him and his siblings, including their immigration from Mexico, and he recognizes the difficult situation his mother is currently in, having to work long hours and drive long distances every day to and from work: "She's usually always driving and she says she gets really tired, because, I mean, those are long hours." Eduardo seems willing to play his part as "role-model child" in the family. He also seems to realize, however, that he does not need to do this on his own, and he seeks out the adult support and guidance he needs to succeed at school. Eduardo has thus successfully forged close relationships with many of his teachers, particularly Mr. Blair and Ms. Alvarez.

As demonstrated in several other student portraits as well as in the focus group interviews, the *Portraits of Promise* students deeply appreciate relationships with teachers that go beyond academics, and they seek relationships with adults with whom they can share some of the problems that affect them outside of school. Researcher Ricardo D. Stanton-Salazar, in his book *Manufacturing Hope and Despair*, delves deeply into the issue of teachers and counselors serving as supportive, informal mentors to students from working-class Mexican immigrant and Mexican American families. Stanton-Salazar and his colleagues studied relationships that students formed through classroom interactions as well as through participation in extracurricular activities, sports teams, and even detention. Like Eduardo, the students in Stanton-Salazar's study had relationships with teachers that provided them with academic support, advice for college, outlets for fun and relaxation, and help in thinking through some of the challenges they faced at home. In synthesizing this aspect of his team's findings from their research at several high schools in Southern California, which included intensive interviews with fifty-one students, Stanton-Salazar reports findings similar to those represented in this book:

> The fondness and emotional attachment many students felt toward key teachers served as important sources of academic motivation and resiliency. Throughout our interviews, the notion that schooling occurs in the context of real human relationships became abundantly evident.[2]

For Eduardo, teacher relationships seem to serve as a sort of lifeline, especially given the difficulties he faces at home and the extra pressure he says his parents place on him to be a role model for his younger brother. Educators must, of course, be aware of maintaining appropriate professional boundaries with students (teachers are not psychologists and guidance counselors are not parents), but Eduardo's story also illustrates some of the ways educators can open their doors to students who, due to various circumstances, may need an extra level of personal and emotional support in order to succeed academically.

Eduardo also clearly takes advantage of peer networks at school to stay on track, something made possible by the fact that, as he puts it, "everyone [students] gets along pretty well." As indicated by the comments of several other students attending both CCS and NYGHS, peer support among high-achieving students at both of these schools is high, and students routinely motivate and help one another to excel. Eduardo can thus be seen as a student who is academically and personally resilient by virtue of his relational connections at school.[3] That is, Eduardo's school relationships seem to protect him in various ways from the risks that might threaten the academic performance of another student under similar circumstances.[4] Although Eduardo's academic confidence, self-advocacy, and intellectual curiosity clearly play important roles in his inclination to seek out such relationships and make a second home of sorts for himself at school, his story suggests the need for educators to consider how they might build the same kind of resilience in students who, due to shyness, lack of English proficiency, or other factors, might be less inclined to do so.

Juanita

"I passed all the Regents. In June, I'm going to take the chemistry one and the Spanish one so I can get an advanced diploma."

Putting in Extra Time to Succeed

WHEN I FIRST met quiet, unassuming Juanita, a nineteen-year-old senior at NYGHS, I was concerned that she might be the kind of student who can go relatively unnoticed at school: shy, polite enough not to draw attention to herself, but perhaps flying too much under the radar to get all her needs met as a learner. Particularly in the case of English-language learners, such "low-profile" students can be at risk for failure after graduation, when their skill deficits become more apparent and they are suddenly faced with the realities of college and an adult world that is less nurturing than the one they have left behind in high school.[1]

Juanita spoke very softly during the opening minutes of our one-on-one interview and seemed a little intimidated by the digital recorder sitting in the middle of the table, even though she said it was all right that I use it. I had not yet examined her transcript, so I had no idea before our interview what Juanita's grades were like. Because she volunteered to participate in an interview project about successful students, I expected her to have passing or perhaps even good grades but was surprised to learn—obviously based on a much too hastily drawn first impression—that she was one of the academic stars of NYGHS:

What are your grades like now?
A and A+.

In what subjects?
All of the subjects.

Once Juanita sees how genuinely impressed I am by her academic success, she opens up and tells me more of her story. Juanita moved with her brother to New York from the Dominican Republic two years and nine months before our interview. She is able to tell me the precise day they arrived, July 8. Prior to coming to the U.S., Juanita had been separated from her mother for seven years, a separation she found "very hard." Now that I know Juanita has such strong grades, I make another false assumption: that she must have known some English before she came to NYGHS.

How much English did you know coming here?
I didn't know any.

You didn't know *any*?
No.

How did that feel, to come here not knowing any English?
I felt like such a stranger, because, you know, I didn't know no one here. I didn't know the English. I didn't have any friends and, like, I felt weird when I get to class. I didn't know what the teacher was talking about. I was nervous.

Next, I ask Juanita to reflect on the things that she believes helped her overcome her initial difficulties at NYGHS. As other students profiled in the portraits did, Juanita mentions relationships with key teachers and students who were willing to work together to help her translate lessons into her native language and thus help her slowly build social confidence in such a strange new context:

> *You know, some teachers, even though they didn't know how to speak Spanish, they put some students that know English and also know Spanish to translate it, so I can know what they were saying and do my work.*

> **Did you know the students you were working with at all?**
> *No, I didn't know them. But after that, you know, I just started making friends.*

LEARNING TO INTEGRATE SOCIAL SKILLS AND ACADEMICS

When Juanita first arrived at NYGHS from the Dominican Republic, she had to learn how to interact at school not only in a new language but also in some ways to which she was unaccustomed. When I ask her to describe the differences between her school in the Dominican Republic, which she left in eighth grade, and school at NYGHS, she begins by describing structural differences in the school day, then delves more deeply into how teacher expectations and interactions with peers are also very different in the two contexts:

> *It is very different, because in D.R. in the school, you know the time— it's just from 8:00 to 12:00. Here it is from 9:00 to 4:00. Here you have to take, like, twelve subjects, and there you just take seven or six. And there you have to, like, give an explanation every single day. And here you don't have to. . . . I was learning very different there—it is very different. And the teachers, they like, they just write on the board and*

they give you the notebook, the books, and you have to, like, go to some page and read about it, and then tomorrow you have to explain this. And here they give you paper and explain it to you and they put you to work in groups, but in D.R. you have to work by yourself.

When I ask Juanita what learning style she prefers, working alone or working in groups, she answers, "Working in groups, because there you have more ideas and it is better."

Like Karla, as profiled earlier, however, Juanita says there is one aspect of learning at NYGHS to which she has still not grown accustomed: portfolio presentation. As a summative assessment at the end of the semester, students at NYGHS are required to present a synthesis of what they have learned in core subjects (e.g., literature, mathematics, history) to a panel. Although Juanita says she is comfortable learning in English now and no longer needs to translate material into Spanish to understand course content, she still finds portfolio presentation daunting, particularly since it requires her to explain complex course concepts in English to an audience:

I don't like portfolio. I don't know. It's like, if you learned something, I don't have to explain it to others, to me I just learned it. If you say, "Can you do this?" [I'd reply], "Yes, I can do it." I don't have to explain it. In portfolio, you have to explain it. . . . I don't know if it's maybe because of the English, because if it's in Spanish, maybe I could explain it.

Despite Juanita's ongoing struggles with portfolio assessment, she has a straight-A transcript. When I ask her to reflect on the factors behind her success, she first credits her mother for urging her to focus on her own learning, even when teachers behave in ways that could cause students to disengage:

Always in my house, before I go to school my mom, when she advises me what I have to do: "You have to listen to the teacher and the school, even though sometimes they raise their voices."

Juanita also echoes many of her *Portraits of Promise* peers in attributing a large portion of her success at school to a combination of her own hard work and the support of her teachers: "I succeed on my own and with the help of the teacher." As Juanita explains, one way she does this is by spending a lot of time with her teachers after school. Juanita estimates that she spends between an hour and an hour and a half every day after school in teachers' classrooms, following up on lessons that took place during the day and clarifying any points about which she might have been confused. Since school at NYGHS ends close to 4:00 p.m. most days, Juanita is often in the building past 5:00:

> *I stay after school for chemistry or U.S. history or math or any class. If you're in the classroom and the teacher is teaching us, if I don't understand something so well, I stay after school so they can explain it better.*

In the roughly two and a half years since she arrived in the United States, Juanita has also passed all the required state Regents exams to graduate (including the English-language arts exam, for which students are not allowed to receive any translated material), and she is planning to take several additional tests in order to receive an advanced diploma:

> *I passed geometry, algebra, English, science, U.S. history, and global. . . . In June, I'm going to take the chemistry one and the Spanish one so I can get an advanced diploma.*

When I ask Juanita why she thinks she has been so successful on the Regents exams, she answers quickly: "Afterschool program." She goes on to explain that NYGHS provides supplemental afterschool preparation for the Regents exams in certain subjects; for other subjects, this preparation is integrated into the school day.

At the time of our interview, Juanita was waiting to hear from twelve colleges to which she had applied, and her first-choice schools were three highly competitive colleges in the New York area. As other students at both NYGHS and CCS did, Juanita relied on her school

counselors and on her advisory class—a course focused on the achievement of students' academic and personal goals—to learn about the college application process, financial aid, and how to put her best foot
forward as an applicant: "In advisory, in this class they help us to get
ready for college, also with the application—this class is especially for
this." Like both Diana and Karla, Juanita is considering pediatrics as a
possible career, and she is planning to take college courses in chemistry
(her favorite class at NYGHS) as well as other fields on a pre-med track:
"I really love kids, because ever since I was in the D.R., I was the one
that takes care of the little baby." When I ask if she is at all concerned
about being ready for college, Juanita—despite the impressive trajectory she has followed in learning English so far—realizes that she will
need to deepen her knowledge of English still more in order to be ready
to engage with high-level college material: "What I think [I might not
be ready for] is the language. Before I start getting into the medical
courses, I'll have to take like two years of English."

Nevertheless, Juanita seems undaunted as she looks ahead, perhaps
because of all she has already accomplished in the last two and a half
years, her mother's exhortations that she remain focused, and her belief
in her own determination and skills. Juanita reluctantly answers in the
affirmative when I ask her if she thinks she is a hard worker, and when
I ask her if she thinks she is smart, at first she laughs and demurs even
more noticeably, but finally offers an answer: "I don't know, but people
tell me, 'You're very smart, Juanita. You can do it!'"

LISTENING TO JUANITA

Listening to Juanita's story, it is apparent that, despite her reluctance
to admit that she is a highly intelligent young woman and a very hard
worker, she arrived at NYGHS with a strong set of academic skills, even
if at first she could not demonstrate them in English. Fortunately for
Juanita, the school seems to have provided her with opportunities to
prove her talents, grow as a learner, and prepare for success in college.

And while Juanita's determination and willingness to put in extra hours with teachers—as well as the strong motivation of her mother—have clearly been important variables contributing to her achievement, school factors seem to have been almost as crucial to her success.

I did not know Juanita when she first arrived at NYGHS, but given her quiet demeanor during the interview process and her description of her first days at the school, it is easy to imagine her having been even quieter—perhaps even withdrawn—when she was completely new to the school and had not yet learned English:

> *I felt like such a stranger, because, you know, I didn't know no one here. I didn't know the English. I didn't have any friends and, like, I felt weird when I get to class. I didn't know what the teacher was talking about. I was nervous.*

Drawing on her work with immigrant children, educator Cristina Igoa describes a "silent stage" that many children go through when they are confronted with the world of U.S. schooling for the first time. As Igoa notes, "In the silent stage, immigrant children may appear to be retiring, moody, fearful, even terrified."[2] While Igoa goes on to explain that the silent stage may confer some advantages to immigrant children as it gives them an opportunity to "become insightful observers of their own human condition and of life around them," it can also put them at risk for being perceived as less capable than they really are.[3] As Evangeline Harris Stefanakis has noted based on her research and work with young immigrant students, immigrant children are likely to be incorrectly referred for special education when they are in U.S. schools for the first time, since educators often have difficulty "finding their strengths," especially if they are extremely quiet due to their initial lack of proficiency in English.[4] Stefanakis goes on to recommend that educators incorporate testing practices aimed at developing students' strengths rather than labeling them as deficient.[5]

Fortunately, Juanita seems to be in a school environment in which her strengths have had ample opportunities to emerge. As numerous other students interviewed for this book have done, Juanita has used her peers effectively as a resource for learning both English (when she was new to the school) and academic content (primarily through group work). In addition, the fact that Juanita spends as much time as she does after school serves as a testament not only to her own determination to succeed but also to the willingness of her teachers to spend significant amounts of time with her outside of regular class time—and to push her to engage with content that is challenging enough to require extra effort. (It is not uncommon to see teachers at NYGHS working with students past 5:00 p.m.)

Perhaps ironically, Juanita seems to have found standardized testing to be an empowering, rather than demoralizing, experience. She beams with pride when she tells me about all the Regents exams she has passed and the fact that she plans to take two additional tests in order to receive an advanced diploma. While numerous scholars have written convincingly and with appropriate concern about the damaging effects high-stakes tests such as the Regents exams in New York can have on both the morale and the future life chances of immigrant students—many of whom are ill-prepared to succeed on the tests due to language difficulties, interruptions in their formal education, and other issues—Juanita seems to be an exception to this pattern.[6] In contrast, she seems to view the Regents exams as a form of valuable U.S. educational capital, a ticket to the world of college and beyond, and her success on these tests serves as proof to her and to others that she is truly an American high school graduate who is ready to move on to the next level in her schooling.

Juanita's plan to attend a four-year college after graduation points to the important role her teachers and counselors—and particularly her advisory class and teacher—have played in her readiness for this next step in her academic career. In providing Juanita with information about various colleges, the application process, and financial aid—as well as the encouragement to aim high in these pursuits—her teachers seem to have worked with her to create what researcher Roberta

Espinoza has called a "pivotal moment" for her future.[7] As Espinoza has noted, these kinds of "pivotal moments" are especially important for low-income students and others whose families lack the educational experience and/or social capital to advocate for their children. Given Juanita's strong academic record, it seems plausible that she might have attended college under any circumstances, but the fact that she has applied to twelve colleges and hopes to attend a competitive four-year school despite having only been in the U.S. for two and a half years speaks to the advocacy and organizational help she has received from her teachers and counselors.

Juanita seems to be the first to recognize, however, that there is more she needs to learn in order to be successful in college, particularly when it comes to English. As numerous researchers have found, even for students with a basic level of functional literacy, it takes at least seven years for them to acquire the necessary English skills they need to do high-level work in various academic disciplines.[8] Juanita's ongoing struggles with portfolio assessment also point to the fact that, although she has achieved an impressive level of proficiency in English so far, she still has considerably further to go. Her story thus highlights the need to provide immigrant students with support for the learning of English not just while they are in K–12 schools but also as they make the transition to college.

Marisol

"Going to college—I don't know. Before, I wanted to. Now, like, I don't know. I just kind of gave up on myself."

At a Crossroads

A FRIENDLY, SOCIABLE, AND OPINIONATED sixteen-year-old, Marisol was an easy student with whom to establish a rapport during my relatively short time at CCS. Candid and forthcoming in her interview, Marisol told me, "I'm an open book—to a point." Marisol says her grades have slipped considerably since eighth grade, but her 3.2 grade point average shows that her promise is still very much alive. She seems to be struggling, though, to maintain her motivation at a time in her life when she feels confused about her future goals and at times wants to "give up" on the idea of college. In a story that parallels that of many other students profiled in the portraits, Marisol draws on support from teachers and peers who put pressure on her to succeed, even when she is not sure what she wants for herself at this crucial stage in her life.

Marisol immigrated from one of Mexico's largest cities at the age of five with her parents and one-year-old sister. She remembers having attended preschool in Mexico and having lived in a large house there with her parents, sister, grandparents, and several extended family members. Marisol's parents were both fieldworkers at the time of their move, and the family has moved six times since their arrival in the United States.

Marisol recalls her first encounter in a U.S. public school as one in which a school official, in an initial meeting with Marisol and her mother, invited her—against her mother's wishes—to change to her middle name or perhaps even another name in preparation for entry into this new school context:

> *I remember the first day of school my mom took me to the office. The lady was like, "Oh, so what's her name?" . . . And the lady was like, "What name do you want?" She was asking me, "What name do you want?" She was asking me, but my mom said, "Marisol." And she [the school official] said, "I'm asking the little girl. What would be better for her, and what would she like to be called?" . . . [After my mother left], she's like, "This is your chance. You can be, like, either/or."*

In most respects, Marisol's first entry into a U.S. elementary school was unlike the experience Diana discusses in her portrait, in which she felt demoralized by teachers and classmates who doubted her academic ability because she was Mexican and could not speak English. If anything, Marisol's first teachers in the U.S. recognized her potential early. Even though Marisol entered kindergarten only a month before the end of the year, her teacher allowed her to graduate and move on to first grade. Marisol's kindergarten teacher did not speak Spanish, but Marisol recalls that she often helped to facilitate connections between Marisol and her classmates who could speak both Spanish and English:

> *Her kids would help me. Like, my classmates would translate what she would be telling me. Even though they were kindergartners, like, they*

would translate what she was telling me. I remember one little girl there, I think her name was Rosemary. Yeah, I think her name was Rosemary, and she would help me a lot. And she was the one that would, like, show me around the school, she'd like, everything, she would help me with everything. . . . The teacher, she helped me out, too, because the teacher would tell her [Rosemary], and then she would tell me. . . . It was kind of weird. I did only a month of kinder [kindergarten], but I still graduated.

Marisol says she spent a lot of time during the summer after kindergarten learning English informally ("like from watching TV and stuff"), and even though she was still not completely proficient in English in first grade, she became one of the top two students in her class. Because of her outstanding skills, Marisol says her teacher would often single out her and one of the high-achieving boys in the class for enrichment and for special, more advanced activities than those in which the rest of the class was participating.

Marisol's family moved frequently during her elementary school years, sometimes living with friends or relatives as her parents sought work. Although the family's frequent moves somewhat disrupted the continuity of Marisol's education in elementary school, she says she was a high achiever all the way through eighth grade: "From first to eighth grade, I have like a lot of awards. Like, every month I would get two or three awards. . . . I have two medals, principal's list, honor roll." By most standards, Marisol is still a high-achieving student, with no grades lower than a C. As it is for many young people, however, adolescence has been a somewhat challenging time in which Marisol has struggled to figure out her current priorities and plans for the future. At least some of this difficulty, as Marisol tells it, stems from conflicts she experiences with her immigrant parents, primarily her mother, who seem to hold different values than those Marisol has as an American adolescent.

MARISOL'S TENSIONS WITH HER FAMILY

One source of family tension that causes Marisol considerable distress, she says, stems from the fact that her mother often compares her to her cousins who live in Mexico. Marisol says her mother often tells her that she wishes Marisol would be more like these cousins—more deferential to authority and behaving in other ways she views as more in keeping with proper values. Marisol sees this comparison as false, however, making the point that she and her cousins were raised in different cultures with different expectations:

> My parents, my mom mostly, she's always like, "You should see your cousins from Mexico, they do this and this and this." And I just say, "I didn't ask to be brought here. You brought me here, so why should I be in trouble for not being the same way that they are? If they are raised in, like, a total different environment, like different rules than what we are like, with different everything—different schedules, everything."

When I follow up by asking Marisol if she wishes her family had stayed in Mexico, she expresses ambivalence:

> It's harder to get an education over there, but they still get it. A lot of people still get it, so it doesn't really matter where. It's just that here it's easier, because it's public, so things are free here. There you have to buy a lot of things, so it's hard. . . . I think it would be the same. Like, I don't really care where I am.

Marisol believes that her relationship with her mother is strained further by a growing educational and linguistic divide between them. Whereas in Marisol's early childhood her mother was able to advocate for her and play a more active role in her education, especially when the family lived in Mexico, Marisol believes her mother is frustrated now because she feels less able to participate in her children's schooling:

> My mom doesn't speak English, she doesn't speak it. I think she stopped going to school when she was like in fifth grade or sixth grade. . . . She

felt bad, like, because, like, my dad came over here first, and she would
be the one helping us out over there [in Mexico]. But now it's like, she
can't help me.

Marisol also feels a cultural tension with her parents around the issue of romantic relationships. Marisol has been hiding the fact that she has a boyfriend from her parents; she says her parents have forbidden it because they believe it would distract her from her schoolwork. Marisol is critical of the special rules her parents seem to have for her just because she is a girl, especially since she says her sister uses her looks to get attention and has already "bought in" to cultural female beauty standards at the expense of her education, even though she is only in fifth grade:

She's like the type that thinks beauty is everything, forget school, and
she's only a fifth-grader. Everybody tells her, "Oh, you're so pretty." And she
makes the little "thank you" face. She's smart, but she doesn't try at all.

Finally, Marisol says the fact that her father has been unable to work recently because of an injury has put a financial strain on the family. Marisol has an afterschool job and, because she recognizes her parents' difficulty, she offers to give her parents all the money she earns. Marisol says her mother refuses to take the money at first but ultimately realizes the family needs the extra funds to help make ends meet. Marisol explains, "I know she needs the money. . . . I don't want money. It's like a bad thing. It makes people go crazy."

The difficulties Marisol has had with family relationships in recent years have led her to doubt whether she even wants to attend college. Her comments suggest that her confusion about her future is, at least in part, due to the fact that she feels she is not getting the level of support from her family that she did in her earlier schooling. Without this formerly secure foundation, Marisol seems unsure about how to proceed:

I know I can handle it [college], but like—From when I was in kinder
[kindergarten] like to eighth-grade year, I had a lot of things, people

helping me. With my teenage years, it's like parents don't help. It's hard to explain. It's not that I can't do the work—I can do the work, I can. . . . I don't know. I'm confused.

THE INTERVENTION OF TEACHERS AND FRIENDS

When Marisol started high school at CCS, she says she was on track toward an academic free fall until she began to receive support from teachers and peers in ways that compensated for the decline in support she felt at home. Ms. Alvarez, Marisol's math teacher, who was mentioned as a supportive mentor by numerous other students I interviewed, is one of several people who are now pushing Marisol to stay focused on academics. In this context Marisol also mentions Juan, another high-achiever who was part of the *Portraits of Promise* interviews, as one of several students who tries to keep her "on track" academically. Many of the students at CCS, including Marisol, call Juan "Governor" because of his physical resemblance to a prominent politician and because of his seriousness and his status as a student leader:

> *Once I started my freshman year, I soon gave up on stuff. Like, "Why should I try to satisfy her [my mother]? If I try, I can't satisfy her, so why do it?" Then Ms. Alvarez start talking to me. She's like, "You better stay in school." And all my friends, like mostly Governor, like Juan, says, "Why are you giving up?" and stuff. "Keep on trying. Do it for yourself. Don't just do it for her [your mother]. Do it for you."*

Marisol has an ongoing banter with Juan about the need for her to stay focused. When her grades slip, Marisol says that Juan will try to cajole her to improve her performance: "He'll say, 'I'm sad, Sister. You have bad grades.' And then he makes me feel bad. And then I pick them up and he says, 'You're my sister again.'" Marisol believes that she, Juan, and another friend of hers named Felipe have formed a sort of support network whereby they motivate one another in school, in part because they receive less support at home than some of their peers: "I think he

[Juan] has the same situation as me and Felipe. . . . We sort of have like the same thing, because I'm not as close to my parents and Felipe isn't close to his parents."[1] In addition to Juan and Felipe, Marisol says she has a former boyfriend who plays an almost parental role in keeping her on track academically: "He goes to my teachers and says, 'If she has lower than a C, call me.'"

When I ask Marisol to look ahead to her future, she says she has "no idea" what she wants to do after graduation. Marisol often takes on responsibility for her family as a "language broker"—she translates documents for them and negotiates transactions in English on their behalf in various public contexts.[2] Because of the skills she has exhibited in this area, Marisol says her mother wants her to be a professional translator. Marisol says she is more interested in studying history, but she even feels unsure about this:

> *I have no idea. My parents want me to be one thing and I want to be something else. . . . Like, I can translate. Like, I can do that really good. Like, I like history a lot. My parents want me to do that, translate papers in Spanish, but I want, like, to study history. Then at the same time I don't know what I want to do. Going to college—I don't know. Before, I wanted to. Now, like, I don't know. I just kind of gave up on myself. I don't know. I know I can. I feel just like—I don't know.*

Marisol still has two and a half more years at CCS to figure out what she wants to do after graduation, so there is reason to hope she will make some positive choices and fulfill her promise in whatever way she chooses. When I ask her about the assets she has now that give her hope as she looks ahead to the future, she mentions the same friends and teachers who have helped guide her in a positive direction so far:

> *My friends and my teachers [give me hope]. I feel hopeful knowing that if I don't get the help I need at my house, I can come and talk to my teachers. Ms. Alvarez—I'm sure you've heard her name like a billion times—she's like an aunt to me.*

LISTENING TO MARISOL

Marisol's story is a departure from those profiled in the other portraits in that, at least at the time she was interviewed, the fulfillment of her promise seemed to be at risk. Although on one level some of Marisol's decrease in motivation and her ambivalence about her future might be attributed to difficulties negotiating the common "crisis" of adolescent identity, specifics of her family situation are also clearly causing her considerable distress.[3]

Marisol's educational history in the United States seems to have begun highly successfully—despite the fact that a school official found it appropriate to "subtract" her name on her first day as a student.[4] After this initial experience, Marisol seems to have thrived (as did other students in these portraits) from the opportunity to learn from peers who spoke both Spanish and English and the willingness of teachers to facilitate these connections. Moreover, Marisol seems to have benefited early from what researchers have called an "anointment effect"— a designation as special or gifted that can spur a student on to further academic success.[5] Marisol fulfilled this expectation of outstanding academic ability all the way through eighth grade, as evidenced by the many awards she received in elementary school.

More recently, however, Marisol believes she has a more and more difficult time pleasing her parents, especially her mother, and getting positive attention from them. Whereas Marisol says her parents were highly involved in her education when she was younger, she believes this has ceased to be the case now that she is in high school. Interestingly, several CCS staff members expressed the view that Marisol's mother is a strict, highly involved parent who checks up often on her daughter's progress. Yet Marisol clearly finds her mother's interventions unhelpful and oppressive: "You [mother] get mad at me when my grades go low, but you don't really, like, try to help me."

Numerous scholars have written about the widening divisions that often occur between immigrant parents and their children who have been raised for all or most of their lives in the United States.[6] The fact that Marisol's parents have struggled financially since their arrival in the U.S. and that her father has had to stop working due to an injury clearly puts strain on the family. The fact that neither of Marisol's parents speaks much English also seems to have placed an increasing distance between them, particularly in the case of Marisol's mother, who used to help her children with schoolwork but, as Marisol tells it, is frustrated that she can no longer do so.

Cultural divides between immigrant parents and their children raised primarily in the United States can be particularly problematic for Latina girls, as several researchers have noted, as traditional Latin American ideals about femininity clash with the outspokenness girls like Marisol sometimes develop as they become Americanized.[7] Marisol seems acutely aware of this as she bridles at the comparisons her mother often makes between her and her Mexican-raised cousins. In addition, Marisol's need to conceal her boyfriend from her parents is reminiscent of a phenomenon seen among Latina girls in other studies, whereby some parents have been found to be especially distrustful of boys for fear that they will force their daughters to be sexually active or, worse, get them pregnant.[8] Although Marisol says her parents' apprehensions about her having a boyfriend are primarily because they want her to remain focused on schoolwork, the family's tensions about this seem to be part of a widening generational and cultural divide between them. (It is interesting in this context that Marisol says her parents do not seem to object as much to her younger sister's behaviors that play up her physical attractiveness, even as these are interfering with her academic performance.)

Regardless of where the tensions between Marisol and her parents reside, she is fortunate to have high levels of support from both teachers and peers at CCS. Since Marisol, for whatever reasons, seems unable to connect in a positive way with her parents about her schoolwork at this stage in her life, she allows her peers and teachers to act, in a sense, *in loco parentis*, to push her and goad her into realizing her academic potential. In this way, Marisol is typical of students in other studies of Mexican American youth who say their peers are "like family," keeping them out of trouble and exhorting them to succeed when they slip.[9]

Marisol's relationship with several friends, especially Juan, seems to share this quality of family—even to the point where he refers to her as his "little sister." Marisol uses similar familial language in describing her relationship with Ms. Alvarez, the math teacher cited by so many other students in the study: "She's like an aunt to me." Especially when students have difficulty, for whatever reason, connecting with parents or other family members at certain points in their lives, it may therefore be important for educators to consider how to help students cultivate these kinds of "familial" relationships at school.

PART THREE

Living Up to the Promise

Recommendations for Classroom and School Practice

THIS BOOK DRAWS on the voices of a very specific subset of students: adolescents (between the ages of twelve and nineteen) born outside the United States who have been successful in two specific U.S. schooling contexts.[1] Its primary goal has been to find out what they believe are the factors that have helped them to succeed as well as those that they think might support them or their peers more effectively. Interviews with teachers, administrators, parents, social service workers, or others who work with and care about immigrant youth might yield quite a different set of ideas than those presented in these pages, and if this were a different kind of project I would complement the student interviews with some of these additional perspectives. Some outstanding comprehensive research studies, many of which are cited in this book, have taken such approaches. Nevertheless, as I state in the introduction, this book has a more singular but no less important purpose: listening to the ultimate experts, the students themselves, about the things that matter most to them and bringing their voices to the foreground. I believe that hearing their enthusiasm, their triumphs, their frustrations, their disappointments, their determination—and the ways in which key relationships have shaped all of these—puts much of the established research in an informative new light. As I have written previously, "If it matters to one young person, then it matters"—and chances are, it matters to other young people as well.[2] Although these particular students from a small number of countries obviously cannot represent immigrant students everywhere, both the consistencies and contrasts in their responses point to a few key implications about the kinds of learning environments that might help all students reach their full potential.

In the opening chapter of this book, I shared advice that the students offered to teachers for working effectively with them and their peers. These ideas, which the students stated quickly at the end of their focus groups, form the starting point for the more detailed recommendations that follow. (See the introduction for a summary of these initial ideas shared in the focus groups.) Listening to students more closely in the one-on-one interviews, I heard a great deal more about the aspects of their school and family lives that they believe make a difference in their ability to excel. With the students' voices in mind, I humbly offer the following list of implications for educational practice that I heard in these in-depth interviews, with an invitation to readers also to draw their own inferences based on what they "hear" in the portraits. Because most of what students discussed in their interviews related to their schools and how aspects of their past or current education either supported or hindered their success, the list of thirteen recommendations that follows relates primarily to factors at the classroom and school levels. There also are distinct roles to be played by parents and students, however, in partnering effectively with educators and advocating the kinds of learning environments that support success. In addition, policies at the local, state, and national levels as well as societal attitudes about immigration all can have tremendous effects on the capacity of immigrant students to thrive at school and in life.[3] I therefore follow this chapter with an afterword in which I discuss some of these broader forces that deeply affect the lives of immigrant youth in the United States.

Recommendations for Classroom and School Practice

1. Facilitate teacher and peer outreach in the early days of U.S. schooling
2. Create space for the use of languages of origin *and* English
3. Respect students' ties to their countries of origin *and* the United States
4. Emphasize resilience, persistence, and high expectations
5. High-stakes tests: If you can't beat them, use them to your advantage
6. Point the way to college
7. Support students as adolescents
8. Be a "special teacher"
9. Foster resistance
10. Support students supporting one another
11. Draw on outside resources
12. Complement the work of families
13. Make time and *have patience*

Like all schools, CCS and NYGHS are unique learning environments, and given the unique population each school serves—recent immigrants in the case of NYGHS and primarily Mexican-origin students living in an agricultural region in the case of CCS—it is clear how some of the success factors implied or explicitly suggested in the *Portraits of Promise* interviews might be fostered in these kinds of communities. It is easy to imagine, for example, peer-to-peer translation in a school such as NYGHS, with its large and varied immigrant population, or a cohesive familial community in a school like CCS, in which students share many aspects of their linguistic backgrounds and family circumstances. Yet none of the recommendations outlined below need be viewed as context-specific. Rather, they represent an invitation to educators working in all kinds of school settings—from large, urban comprehensive high schools to small, rural community schools—to consider how they might help their own immigrant students, even if they are relatively few in number, to succeed in similar ways. Although some ideas may require modification from the specific ways they play out at CCS or NYGHS, how might educators in all kinds of schools facilitate the relationships, practices, structures, opportunities, and communities that the *Portraits of Promise* students associate with their success?

1. Facilitate Teacher and Peer Outreach in the Early Days of U.S. Schooling

Regardless of whether it took place in early elementary school or in high school, the students' initial entry into U.S. schooling was, for all who remembered it, a crucial moment. Participants spoke poignantly about their deep feelings of disorientation as lessons were being taught and social relationships were being played out in a language they could neither speak nor understand. The New York students used words such as "frustrated" (Omar and Karla), "nervous" (Juanita), and "terrible" (Ibrahim) to describe some of their initial feelings as they struggled to acclimate to NYGHS, a school specifically designed to meet the needs of new immigrant students. It is impossible to know how these students might have fared had they attended a high school with a population more typical of U.S. schools, but it is easy to imagine these feelings of disorientation having been even more intense. For Diana, who immigrated at a much younger age than the New York students, her initial feelings of disorientation were combined with a sense—based on overt messages from both her teacher and her peers—that she was not welcome at her new school. As a result, the most salient feeling for her in her initial weeks of schooling in the United States seems to have been homesickness: "I didn't want to be here. I didn't. I just wanted to go back."

All these young people eventually found a place for themselves as students in the United States and became highly engaged in—and in some cases extremely enthusiastic about—their schools and the learning taking place within them. Although some of this change could obviously be attributed to their own determination, their ability to adapt, and simply the passage of time, connections with both teachers and peers played critical roles in these students' success in their early days of U.S. schooling. In some cases, teachers worked closely and directly with students as they faced the initial struggles of learning English, translating parts of what they were teaching into the students' languages of origin, even if they were drawing on a very basic knowledge of Spanish or another language. In other cases, teachers provided the time, space, and structures such that students could have their peers help them understand lessons and course content. Regardless of who was doing the translating, the *Portraits of Promise* students echoed one another repeatedly in saying that these kinds of connections helped them establish a new relationship to U.S. schooling based not on fear and alienation but on their own ability to excel.

Teacher and peer outreach to newly immigrated students can take many forms in different classroom and school contexts, so it is difficult to make specific recommendations about the practices that might be most effective in this regard. These portraits suggest across the board, however, that targeted and consistent efforts to build bridges of understanding for newly immigrated students, which take into account the frustration and disorientation they may be experiencing, can go a long way toward tapping into talents that may be hidden behind initial linguistic and cultural barriers. They further suggest that both teachers and peers (even children, as in Marisol's case, as young as kindergartners) can serve as crucial assets in this regard.

2. Create Space for the Use of Languages of Origin *and* English

In all the cases in which teachers and peers helped the *Portraits of Promise* students move beyond their initial difficulties, language was paramount, both English and the students' languages of origin. As Karla indicated, just having a teacher translate individual words and phrases into Spanish made a significant difference in a situation in which everything else was new, and peer translation in student groups gave students like Omar and Marisol a sense of grounding in an otherwise completely foreign English-language classroom. Obviously, this translation was key to helping the students understand instruction, but it also helped them build relationships that served as a catalyst toward a positive academic trajectory. As Juanita explained, her early connections with peers, in which she received translation from the other Dominican and Spanish-speaking students in her classes, led to friendships that have been important throughout her years at NYGHS. Similarly, Karla's connections with the other Honduran students in her ninth- and tenth-grade classes led in turn to her meeting older Honduran students, who were able to help her with her homework by discussing it in the specific dialect of Spanish she could understand well. For Diana, the willingness of her second U.S. teacher to allow her to work both in Spanish and English helped forge a teacher-student relationship that served as a foundation for Diana's belief in her ability, not only to fit in, but to excel academically in a U.S. school context.

The opportunities these students were given to speak their native languages while also learning and working in English seem to have had different meanings for students as they spent more time in the United States. While at first teacher and peer translation of class material helped students acquire a basic level of understanding, as students learned more English and relied less on translation, their use of native languages developed more social significance. For the NYGHS students, the use of native languages in social spaces such as the cafeteria provided a reprieve from learning and working in English, which, even as they mastered this skill, could create stress. For the CCS students, most of whom are fluent English speakers, Spanish provided a vital connection to their families as well as their peers, many of whom also speak Spanish at home.

Students' continued use of their native languages, however, seems in no way to have diminished their belief in the importance of learning English to succeed both in high school and in American society. Ibrahim reiterated this notion multiple times during his interview: "You really need to speak English to succeed. English is like the number-one language. You want to speak it." Ibrahim and other students thus corroborate evidence found in prior studies that suggests allowing students to use their native languages diminishes neither their ability to learn English nor their enthusiasm for doing so.[4] As Portes and Rumbaut have noted, immigrants' use of their native languages once they are in the United States need not be perceived, as it is by many English-only advocates, as a "zero-sum" process; there is no "necessary trade-off" between English and any other language.[5] It is beyond the scope of this book to make recommendations about specific, established protocols for the use of multiple languages in education such as English as a Second Language (ESL) or the various types of bilingual programs, since the *Portraits of Promise* students did not discuss these during their interviews. From their perspectives, opportunities for frequent peer collaboration, such as the work groups that exist in many of the classrooms at NYGHS, seem to be a critical variable in the successful use of multiple languages to facilitate learning. The students' comments also suggest that this peer collaboration and translation need to be monitored closely by educators, however, to ensure that they remain productive and that students from "low-incidence populations," those whose languages are not widely represented at school, are not excluded.[6] Overall, the students' experiences seem to be in keeping with the observation of researcher-educators Sonia Nieto and Patty Bode, who suggest that the use of students' native languages and cultures in a variety of creative ways is key to fostering success among immigrant students: "[E]ffective pedagogy is not simply teaching subject areas in another language, but instead finding ways to use the language, culture, and experiences of students meaningfully in their education."[7]

3. Respect Students' Ties to Their Countries of Origin *and* the United States

As Nieto and Bode suggest, and as the *Portraits of Promise* students articulated in various ways, even as students desire to become acculturated to American society, their countries and cultures of origin continue to be highly significant in their lives. As is the case with languages, strong identification with being American and connection to one's country of origin are not mutually exclusive. In their interviews, students expressed feelings about the countries they left behind ranging from Diana's love of Mexico to Ibrahim's sadness about "losing his roots" in Togo. In addition, both New York and California students expressed strong desires to provide financial and other kinds of help to family members and others in their countries of origin.

Some students seemed unsure about whether they wanted to remain in the United States after they finished their education. Omar's desire to go back and forth between the United States and Burkina Faso and Karla's wish to practice medicine in Honduras demonstrate that, even if students believe that the United States affords them better educational and economic opportunities than their countries of origin, their native countries have other things to offer that the U.S. does not. It would therefore be false for educators to assume that an immigrant student's sole aspiration is to become as much like native-born American students as quickly as possible. Rather, these students seem to aspire to what Portes and Rumbaut have called *selective acculturation*, whereby adolescents retain key aspects of their language and culture even as they simultaneously acculturate to being American.[8]

The relatively small number of interviews conducted for this study, combined with the lack of a comparison group, makes it impossible to state with certainty whether the maintenance of ties to native cultures serves as an academic asset for these successful students, but Portes and Rumbaut have associated selective acculturation with families' improved ability to guide and support students' academic success.[9] As is the case for language, then, there may well be benefits to incorporating students' native cultures into their educational experience in meaningful ways. Again, it is beyond the scope of this book to recommend specific pedagogies not discussed by the students, but as Nieto and Bode have also noted, efforts to incorporate students' cultures into their learning should go beyond the "heroes and holidays" approaches to multiculturalism found in many schools, whereby such incorporation can seem token and patronizing.[10] Given the rich life experiences of students who have lived in two cultures (or perhaps more), the possibilities for using these experiences to enhance the learning of both immigrant students and their native-born peers—through writing exercises, class discussions, exhibitions, and other means—are virtually limitless.

4. Emphasize Resilience, Persistence, and High Expectations

As discussed previously, many of the students believed that their own hard work and persistence were the primary reasons why they were successful. At the same time, these high-achieving students recognized that not all their peers were able to sustain the same level of drive or optimism. At NYGHS, students saw their peers struggle, and some give up, when faced with the demands of learning in a new language and completing high-stakes tasks such as the Regents exams and portfolio presentations. At CCS, Ricky saw his peers falter in the absence of the parental encouragement from which he benefited, and Marisol said she struggled to sustain her good grades in part because her family, due to language barriers and other factors, became less able over time to support her progress. Overall, these stories point to a need for educators to encourage and foster academic resilience in students from immigrant families, who face a variety of specific challenges that at times may seem insurmountable, and to encourage them to persist in the face of setbacks such as a failed Regents exam or a dip in grades that may be related to language or other issues.

At the same time, the students seemed to appreciate being held to high standards and expectations. In none of the interviews did students complain that the work they were being asked to do was too difficult (except perhaps in the case of portfolio presentations at NYGHS). Omar and Karla both mentioned Ms. Sheila as a teacher whose high expectations they appreciated, even if at first they shared their peers' opinion that her demands were too high. (Karla: "She put a lot of pressure on us, and she knows what she's doing.") The students at CCS appreciated the opportunity to take college-level courses as well as meet the high standards of their most demanding CCS teachers. In a similar vein, the comments of Ibrahim and Omar about school discipline at NYGHS are noteworthy. Although none of the students who experienced corporal punishment in their countries of origin believed it should be implemented at NYGHS, they did suggest that classroom management in some of their courses could be more effective and motivating. (Ibrahim: "[In Africa] if you talk and talk, and the teacher says you be quiet, that's it. . . . Here, all you got to do is just ignore the teacher and just keep talking. Nothing is going to happen.")

Numerous researchers have noted that many teachers tend to underestimate the capabilities of students from immigrant families because of language issues and false assumptions about their family and/ or educational backgrounds.[11] Many adolescent students in their day-to-day classroom demeanor may project relatively little interest in being pushed by their teachers to work hard and may appear more inclined to socialize with their peers than to focus on math, history, literature, or some other subject. (They are, after all, adolescents.) The *Portraits of Promise* interviews illustrate, however, that at least these successful students want their teachers to insist on excellence, even if the messages they receive from students suggest a different agenda. Both Ricky and Eduardo reported spending hours on their own doing extra academic work beyond that which was assigned, examples of the kind of strong intrinsic motivation on which teachers can capitalize.

5. High-Stakes Tests: If You Can't Beat Them, Use Them to Your Advantage

The potentially damaging effects of using standardized tests for high-stakes purposes such as graduation and promotion from one grade to the next have been well documented.[12] For example, students who are retained in a grade based on their performance on a standardized test have been found to be more likely to drop out of school than other students.[13] As discussed in the previous section, such testing can be especially daunting for English-language learners, especially if they are required to take the tests in English and/or are forced to adapt to a form of testing to which they are unaccustomed relatively soon after their arrival in the United States. Standardized tests required for graduation such as the Regents exams in New York and the California High School Exit Examination (CAHSEE) have the potential to destroy the morale of students who fail them multiple times for reasons associated with limited English proficiency or other factors.[14]

Except in cases in which schools have received testing waivers for various reasons, teachers and administrators have largely been forced to accept these high-stakes tests as a fact of life, and so, in turn, have their students.[15] Yet the experiences of some of the *Portraits of Promise* students suggest that these tests need not be a demoralizing experience for everyone involved. Both Ibrahim and Juanita seem to view the Regents exams in a positive light (at the time of her interview, Juanita was planning to take extra tests to receive an advanced diploma) and to view their scores as proof of their legitimacy as U.S. high school graduates. Moreover, Omar's score of 98 on the U.S. history Regents exam proves that an English-language learner who has only been in the United States for a few years can excel on such assessments. (Because the California students were younger, issues related to standardized tests to meet graduation requirements were much less salient to this group.)

The NYGHS students, especially Juanita, placed a high value on the preparation for standardized tests that was provided at their school and saw it as one of the key factors in their success on these exams. Of course, it is important to consider the benefits of this focus on test preparation alongside the struggles and disappointments associated with standardized testing mentioned previously (as may even have been the case for the high achievers profiled here before they had honed their test-taking skills). Nevertheless, these student portraits suggest that—assuming standardized tests are a necessary reality—educators should develop strategies not only to prepare immigrant students to pass them but to use the tests as opportunities to build students' academic confidence.

6. Help Pave the Way to College

None of the students interviewed for *Portraits of Promise* had parents who had experienced higher education in the United States, and only a few mentioned family members who preceded them in going to college. While this is by no means true for all immigrant youth, some of whom come to the U.S. with highly educated parents who work in various professions, most of the students who participated in this project plan to be trailblazers, the first in their families to go to college in the United States, and in many cases anywhere.[16]

Given that most of the students' families have lacked the opportunity to attend college previously, the students as a group have had limited access to the knowledge base associated with college attendance that many U.S.-born students take for granted.[17] As a result, the connections they make in school and elsewhere that help them understand college applications, options, and financial aid are crucial to their being able to take this next step in their families' upward educational mobility.

Students interviewed for this book discussed a wide variety of supports, from formal programs to informal advising, that they said were crucial in helping them understand what it takes to apply to, be accepted by, and succeed in college. Eduardo, for example, discussed how his advisory teacher helped students weigh the pros and cons of different college majors and professions, while his math teacher helped him figure out the courses he would need as prerequisites to meet his college aspirations. Eduardo had also taken two college-level courses so far through a special program offered by his school. Students at NYGHS, who were closer to college age at the time of their interviews than the California students, learned about the college application process, financial aid, and options for college attendance in their advisory classes, and each had a teacher assigned to them to coordinate their college recommendations. In addition, Karla was one of several NYGHS students who had the opportunity to attend Pathway to College, a program on a suburban campus that made her feel ready for and excited about the college application process. The mere fact that Juanita, less than three years after arriving in the U.S. and learning English, applied to twelve colleges, including several competitive four-year schools, speaks to the value of her school's formal and informal approaches to helping students pursue higher education in the United States.

Juanita's recognition of the need for her to continue learning English even as she applies to college also shows an awareness of the reality she and her peers will face when they graduate from the relatively nurturing world of NYGHS. Many colleges have minimum score requirements on the Test of English as a Foreign Language (TOEFL) and similar exams, and some require that students who are still learning academic English take additional courses to support their English-language development. Literacy scholars estimate that it takes English-language learners between seven and ten years to develop the skills required to perform academic work in English commensurate with their grade and skill levels.[18] In order to help students truly achieve at their level of promise, educators must support English-language learning as an ongoing process, not one that is simply necessary for students when they are new to the country.

7. Support Students as Adolescents

Marisol's story vividly illustrates that adolescents from immigrant families are, first and foremost, adolescents. As widely cited psychologist Erik Erikson noted in his classic writings about youth development during the mid-twentieth century, adolescence is perhaps the time in life when questions about one's identity are most salient to young people.[19] Although these questions are largely explored subconsciously, adolescents—because of the many ways in which this period of life represents a crossroads between childhood and adulthood—are inclined to wonder: "Who am I?" "How do others see me?" "What kind of student do I want to be?" "What things are possible for me in the future?" "Where do I want to go with my life?"[20]

In one sense, this kind of exploration is virtually universal among adolescents. In another sense, however, the adolescent journeys of the students profiled in this book are deeply affected in different ways by the fact that they have grown up in immigrant families. For Marisol, this means negotiating conflicts with her family around gender roles and expectations that she behave like her Mexican cousins. For Ibrahim, it means learning how to honor his roots as both a Togolese African and a Muslim while dealing with the prejudices he faces in the United States about these aspects of his identity. For Omar, it means keeping his focus on schooling and not succumbing to the peer pressure associated with gangs and other risks to which immigrant boys can be especially vulnerable as they acculturate to being American.[21]

Given the varied nature of these experiences, it is difficult to prescribe specific approaches to helping students negotiate the complexities of adolescent identity as they experience them through the specific circumstances of immigration. Peer support groups in which students can talk about the personal issues they face in a safe environment have been shown in other research to make a difference in this regard, helping students build resilience in the face of conditions that might predict risk.[22] Another key factor for many of the *Portraits of Promise* students was the support of teachers—or, in many cases of an individual teacher—on whom they could rely not only for academic help but also for support in dealing with a variety of issues they face outside school.

8. Be a "Special Teacher"

In conversation after conversation, I heard students speak to the deep appreciation they felt for individual teachers who took extra steps to help them with schoolwork, translate material for them, advise them on the college application process, help them find hidden talents, and otherwise encourage them to realize their promise. In many cases, these teachers' outreach to students went beyond academics, with teachers serving as what mentoring researcher Jean Rhodes and her colleagues have called "natural mentors," nonparent adults who serve as role models and provide youth with emotional support, guidance for the future, and opportunities to talk and think through challenges outside the structure of a formal mentoring program.[23] In their research, Rhodes and her colleagues have asked participants to use the following criteria to identify those who qualify as mentors in their lives:

(a) you can count on this person to be there for you, (b) he or she believes in you and cares deeply about you, (c) he or she inspires you to do your best, and (d) knowing him or her has really influenced what you do and the choices that you make.[24]

At CCS, students repeatedly mentioned Ms. Alvarez as a teacher to whom they could turn for such support. Eduardo cited Ms. Alvarez as one of a handful of teachers who guide his thinking about college, serve as a sounding board for difficulties he is facing at home, and provide a space where he can simply "just have fun, talk, and laugh" in the company of an adult. When Marisol's grades started to slip and she seemed to be at serious academic risk, she says Ms. Alvarez told her, "You better stay in school," and helped her make the right choices to get back on track. Marisol speaks in familial terms about Ms. Alvarez and clearly appreciates the extent to which she cares about her future: "She's like an aunt to me."

As the students at NYGHS articulated, one of the factors that makes relationships with individual teachers especially meaningful is longevity, another factor that Rhodes and her colleagues have found to be a key ingredient in an effective mentoring relationship.[25] Ibrahim's relationship with Ms. Elizabeth, for example, seems to hold special meaning for him in that she continues to be someone to whom he can turn for help and advice nearly two years after he has left her class. For Omar, high-quality relationships with teachers involve those who "really listen" to him and his peers, in comparison to other teachers who, he believes, only pretend to do so. Implied in the words of Omar and some of his classmates is the belief that at least some of their teachers underestimate their intelligence, perhaps because they are immigrants and speak English with grammatical imperfections or accents, so they are especially appreciative of teachers who recognize the full range of their abilities and needs. And, as Juanita and Karla state, special teachers are those who guide them through the college planning and application process, providing what researcher Roberta Espinoza has called "pivotal moments" in the direction of their lives, especially if they have relatively few other resources available to them for understanding what it takes to get into college in the United States.[26]

Finally, for those students who immigrated in early elementary school, special teachers were those who saw their potential and took extra time to help them move past their initial disorientation and struggles to learn a brand-new language. Nearly a decade later, Diana vividly recalls the efforts of her second teacher in the United States, who saw her potential and who she says spent many extra hours to help put her on a path toward success: "After I went to second grade, he stopped teaching. But I will always remember him." Research has demonstrated that teacher-mentors can play critical roles in the lives of adolescents from all backgrounds, but the *Portraits of Promise* interviews suggest there may be specific ways these relationships can be beneficial for students who are English language learners and/or come from immigrant families.

9. Foster Resistance

Diana's experience with a special teacher who believed in her potential and spent extra time helping her to realize it clearly helped put her on a positive trajectory in her early schooling. Ironically, Diana said that the demoralizing words and actions of her first teacher in the United States, who openly expressed racist and anti-Mexican attitudes, also contributed to her being the outstanding student she is today in that they motivated her to prove this teacher, and others who think like her, wrong. Clearly, Diana had both internal and external assets that allowed her to turn a highly negative experience, one that might have permanently damaged the self-esteem and academic trajectory of another student, into a motivation to excel. The influence of Diana's parents, both in reinforcing her belief in her abilities and in advocating for her when circumstances threatened it, is evident throughout her story.

Although the behavior of Diana's first teacher in this scenario was extremely unprofessional and, one might hope, unusual among educators who work with young children, it is unfortunately typical of the sort of racist and anti-immigrant attitudes that many immigrant youth encounter at some point in their lives, whether inside or outside of school. Ibrahim has faced harassment for reasons associated with both his ethnicity and his religion and says he no longer feels safe wearing traditional African or Muslim clothing on the streets of New York. Although both CCS and NYGHS seem to be nurturing environments in which the *Portraits of Promise* students perceive little racism or conflict based on students' cultures or languages of origin, it seems likely that most will face encounters with racism and/or anti-immigrant sentiments in some form in college, the workforce, or society after they graduate. It is therefore imperative to help immigrant youth—especially those who may not receive the necessary reinforcement at home—develop the personal strength to maintain their deeply held beliefs in their abilities and in the possibilities for their futures in the face of these challenges.

Although not pertaining directly to the issues that affect immigrant youth, some recent writings by feminist education scholars can be instructive in thinking about how fostering resistance to societal prejudices, oppression, and discrimination can help young people not only put these circumstances in perspective but perhaps even use them, as in Diana's case, to fuel their motivation.[27] Drawing on the writing of Alice Pitt, researcher Janie Victoria Ward defines *resistance* as "the refusal to accept the relevance of certain knowledge to oneself."[28] This refusal is evident in Diana's attitude about the teachers and peers who doubted her ability because she was Mexican ("I wasn't going to let them tell me what I was capable of"), and she acts on this refusal by becoming an academic achiever. In addition to the more personal resistance that Diana exemplifies, researchers have documented ways that educators can help students build their resistance to oppressive societal forces through the study of immigrant history or through involvement in service-oriented projects aimed at effecting political change, particularly as it might be related to causes that affect immigrant youth.[29] As Ward and other educators have noted, it is important in any effort to educate students about issues that affect a particular group (e.g., immigrants) to help students see past a perception of the group as victims and instead to ensure that they have the means to express their resistance productively and can envision ways to effect change.[30] Such expressions of resistance can take many forms, from writing and performance (e.g., theater, music, or spoken-word events), to collective action with peers (e.g., volunteer work, letter-writing campaigns, involvement in political campaigns or protests), to simply making a decision to excel in opposition to low expectations or stereotypes.[31]

10. Support Students Supporting One Another

One of the most inspiring things I heard in the *Portraits of Promise* interviews was the extent to which students supported one another and cheered their peers on to achieve academic success. This was evident in the relationships among peers at CCS, where, for example, Ricky translated lessons for students new to the school and Juan lovingly pressured his "sister" Marisol to bring up her grades and "do it for [her]self." At NYGHS, peer support took the form of more experienced English speakers helping with homework or translating class instructions and materials for their younger and/or less English-proficient peers. In addition, Karla sacrificed spending time on an activity she enjoyed, playing soccer, in order to help one of her peers who was struggling to pass her portfolio assessments and the Regents exams.

The prevalence of peer support for the *Portraits of Promise* students was in keeping with prior research that has found high-achieving immigrant students often rely on their peers for academic motivation and support.[32] Although the peer support among this group clearly speaks to the admirable qualities these students possess and their intrinsic desire to help one another without prompting from teachers, the benefits that accrue from such cooperation make it worth considering how educators can foster peer-to-peer support networks in their schools.

Both CCS and NYGHS are small school communities of fewer than four hundred students. As Eduardo states, "everyone gets along pretty well" at CCS, and friendships at NYGHS cross linguistic and cultural boundaries regularly. As Omar explains, "I don't see who I'm not friends with at this school . . . Spanish, Africans, Arabs, everybody." It is obviously beyond the capability of school-based professionals to change the size or composition of their student populations, but the *Portraits of Promise* interviews suggest that there may be some benefit to the creation of small, cohesive communities within any existing school structure. Both CCS and NYGHS have advisory programs, whereby students meet in small settings designed to promote community-building, goal-setting, preparation for college, and other aspects of success that are important but fall outside traditional classroom disciplines. NYGHS's multiyear groupings, whereby students in ninth and tenth grades and in eleventh and twelfth grades stay together in many of their core subject classes for two years, facilitate the kinds of strong, long-term relationships (both student-to-teacher and peer-to-peer) that promote academic engagement and success.[33] In addition, in both schools peer-centered instruction is an important aspect of classroom practice: peer collaboration takes place frequently in many CCS classrooms, and virtually every classroom at NYGHS is organized into work tables that encourage same-language translation in the lower grades and cross-cultural interaction in the upper grades.

11. Draw on Outside Resources

Numerous students in both the New York and California interviews mentioned experiences that took place outside the normal school day as especially influential in their path toward success. Ibrahim spoke effusively about the extra help he received in the Newcomer Youth Resource Alliance program for learning English and building his academic skills as well as the fun he had participating through NYRA in a variety of experiences such as drama. Omar credits the City Match program with introducing him to many rich experiences around New York and providing him with an outlet to relieve academic stress and "get [his] mind relaxed." The Pathway to College program not only educated Karla about the college application process but gave her the opportunity to stay on a college campus for several days and interact with peers from other schools. For CCS students, the opportunity to take college courses provided them a window into the demands and expectations of postsecondary learning, and the science and college fairs that students such as Diana and Ricky attended helped give them a sense of the larger world outside their schools so that they could ultimately envision the possibilities for themselves after their graduation from CCS.

Youth development theorists have described the benefits of such experiences in many ways, but virtually all agree that activities which serve to expand the horizons of young people—especially those without the family resources to seek out such expansion for themselves— are extremely beneficial during adolescence. Child and adolescent psychology pioneer Erik Erikson referred to these as "moratorium" experiences, occurring at a time in adolescence "during which the young adult through free role experimentation may find a niche in some section of his society."[34] Youth development scholar and program director Michael Nakkula has highlighted the importance of "creating possibility" for young people beyond what their immediate socioeconomic circumstances might afford them.[35] And researchers Markus and Nurius have written about the importance of young people having opportunities to imagine "possible selves."[36] The common notion connecting all of these concepts is the benefit of youth having opportunities to look beyond their immediate surroundings to the range of possibilities both in their environment and within themselves. Especially given the racist and anti-immigrant attitudes many of these young people encounter, as discussed previously in recommendation 9, having an expansive sense of possibility for one's future seems critical. Although the availability of programs and resources outside schools obviously varies from region to region, these interviews suggest that connecting students to available resources and programs can help educators build on whatever beneficial programming is also taking place within the school building.

12. Complement the Work of Families

Past research has indicated that many immigrant parents place a high value on education, and they pass these beliefs on to their children in the form of messages at home about the importance of school and consistent encouragement to work hard and aim high in their ambitions.[37] Despite this fact, researchers have also found that many teachers, school administrators, and non-immigrant parents believe that immigrant parents are relatively uninvolved in their children's education.[38] Teachers often misconstrue parents' absences at school events or disinclination to call them as a lack of interest, when these things in fact may have more to do with language barriers or prohibitive working hours.[39] In addition, educators sometimes inaccurately perceive the family responsibilities that many immigrant youth take on (such as Omar's care for his five-year-old sister) as evidence that the family and/ or student does not view education as a high priority.[40]

The *Portraits of Promise* interviews revealed no shortage of parental interest, but they did point to several challenges students' parents faced in playing active roles in their education. Stories like Eduardo's exemplified how many immigrant parents work long hours and may therefore have difficulty attending school events. The vast majority of students, when asked about college, expressed concerns about their families' ability to pay for it, since most of their parents faced considerable financial struggles. Moreover, most of the students interviewed at both sites indicated that their parents were not able to discuss or help with homework in any specific ways because they speak little or no English. Nevertheless, most of the students' stories illustrated clearly and poignantly how they had internalized their parents' values of hard work and the importance of education, and many spoke with gratitude about the sacrifices their parents have made in moving to the U.S. so they could have better educational opportunities. Even among parents of modest financial means, some students mentioned material support their parents provided to them, as exemplified by Ricky's statement: "My parents always do whatever they can to help me out, whether it's buy me something important . . . transport me somewhere, like to a college tour or like field trips." Perhaps most important, many students (something indicated most clearly in the California focus group) believed that the support they received from their parents—even though it did not usually come in the form of financial assistance or specific help with classwork—was the most important factor, beyond their own hard work, in their success.

These accounts suggest that there may exist opportunities for educators to capitalize on the support many immigrant parents provide to their children at home. In her book *Con Respeto: Bridging the Distances Between Culturally Diverse Families and Schools*, researcher and educator Guadalupe Valdés highlights three general approaches that schools take in their work with parents: *parent involvement*, which usually focuses on reaching out to parents so that they can participate more fully in their children's schoolwork and in interactions with teachers and the school; *parent education*, which involves efforts on the part of school staff to influence home-based parenting practices that educators believe support school success; and, less commonly, *parent empowerment*, programs generally aimed at helping immigrant parents understand the education system and how to serve as effective advocates for their children within it.[41] As Valdés goes on to point out, all of these approaches are aimed, in one way or another, at changes that can be risky in that they affect a child's most important support system:

> *Programs that are directed at families, whether they involve parent education, bringing about parent involvement, or fomenting parent*

empowerment, are, in essence, interventionist. They are designed to change families.[42]

The *Portraits of Promise* students view their parents, despite the fact that they have low incomes and can speak little or no English, as their primary relational assets. Therefore, while it is beyond the scope of this book to recommend one parent engagement approach over another, an overriding message heard in the interviews is that family-based support and school-based support should work in complementary ways in the lives of immigrant students, with neither domain imposing its values or approaches on the other. Even if immigrant parents are not helping with homework, what messages are they sending (perhaps daily) that a teacher can reinforce, complement, and perhaps make more academically tangible for a student? Beginning with this level of awareness as a foundation, it seems plausible that potentially effective parent-educator alliances can be formed and schools and families can learn to work as partners such that, as Omar describes, "[It's] all working in the same direction."

13. Make Time and *Have Patience*

I would be remiss in offering this list of recommendations without re-iterating the idea that was repeated most frequently in both the focus groups and individual interviews: patience. Even these successful students thought teachers could be more patient with them and their peers, especially given the challenges some of them have faced adjusting to learning in a new language and culture.

Overall, these interviews indicate that one of the most valuable commodities—if not the most valuable commodity—we can provide to immigrant students is time. The value of time is evident in Juanita's commitment to spending between one and a half and two hours after school every day to seek clarification on classroom lessons; in the willingness of Eduardo's teachers to talk with him not only about academics but also about issues he is facing at home; in the efforts of Karla's biology teacher to translate words for her and teach her English grammar outside the science classroom. Although there was no comparison group for these interviews, it may well be that immigrant students—particularly those for whom English is not a first language—need more time with teachers and their peers than native-born students in order to succeed academically. At both CCS and NYGHS, teachers clearly provided this time generously, yet it may be important to think in more structural terms about how school policies might be shaped such that all immigrant students could benefit from having the time they need—both on their own and with their peers and teachers—to realize their promise.

A Culture of Promise?

THE LATE PSYCHOLOGIST and Head Start co-founder Urie Bronfenbrenner focused much of his work in the latter part of the twentieth century on understanding the complex ecologies of children's lives. In response to psychological research based largely on studies of individual children and their responses to stimuli in isolated or, at most, two-person laboratory situations, Bronfenbrenner argued that young people's lives could only be understood and therefore improved if examined in broader, real-world contexts. Going further, he noted that children are strongly influenced not only by the aspects of their surroundings with which they come into immediate contact—such as their schools, families, and peer groups—but by broader forces they may never see but that nonetheless have a strong impact on their lives. Effecting change in individual children's life trajectories, then, requires changes not only of "micro-level" factors such as those that exist in schools, neighborhoods, and homes but also of "macro-level" forces such as government policies and the very values and beliefs that permeate society.[1]

Many of the researchers cited in previous sections of this book have recommended policy changes to improve the lives of immigrant children and adults living in the United States and have addressed these issues in a comprehensive way.[2] The focus here is on a narrower set of four issues prompted by themes that emerged in the *Portraits of Promise* interviews. In addition to changes in schools, families, and peer groups, what would American society look like if it were to nurture fully the

147

promise represented by the intelligent, capable, and caring young people like those whose voices are heard in this book?

First, the neighborhoods in which they live and attend school would be safe. Unfortunately, the concerns that Ibrahim and Omar expressed about safety in their neighborhoods do not reflect an isolated set of experiences. Immigrant youth are considerably more likely than their U.S.-born peers to live in segregated urban neighborhoods with high concentrations of poverty.[3] Gary Orfield and his colleagues at the Civil Rights Project have noted that many immigrant youth experience "triple segregation" in their schools and neighborhoods, segregation related not only to poverty but also to skin color and language.[4] Poverty in urban neighborhoods often coexists with dysfunctional schools that serve immigrant students poorly and with factors such as gang activity and drug trade, which pose obvious risks to their safety and well-being.[5] In addition to the stress that feeling unsafe causes students like Omar and Ibrahim, which has the potential to distract them from the already difficult task of learning in a new language and school context, many immigrant young people succumb to risky behaviors and situations endemic to poor urban neighborhoods as a way of fitting in, and boys may be especially vulnerable in this regard.[6] In order to fulfill the promise that all bright, motivated immigrant youth possess, we should do everything we can to ensure that they live and attend school in safe places.

As described by the New York students profiled here, NYGHS— with its multifaceted approach to preparing students for college and its nurturing, cross-cultural community—serves as an oasis of sorts within a high-poverty area of the city, but as the students explain, its ability to protect them from some of the risks of their neighborhoods is limited. Moreover, research suggests that the comprehensive focus on immigrant students at NYGHS is exceptional and does not reflect the experiences of many immigrant youth who attend large urban high schools around the nation, where they are often either segregated in substandard programs or left to fend, academically and socially, largely for themselves among their native-English-speaking peers.[7]

Of course, getting immigrant youth out of neighborhoods with high concentrations of poverty means that, *second, their families would be able to earn more than a subsistence-level living.* Household incomes for immigrant families are significantly lower on average than for the U.S.-born population, and immigrants from three countries represented in the *Portraits of Promise* interviews—Honduras, Mexico, and the Dominican Republic—have poverty rates approaching 30 percent, nearly twice that of native-born U.S. families.[8] Despite the perception that immigrants and their children come to the United States and take jobs away from Americans, the reality is that immigrant adults often work long hours in physically demanding, low-paying jobs, like those "in the fields" held by many of the parents of CCS students. Moreover, the decision of many immigrant parents to work in the United States is prompted not simply by their own initiative to seek a better life but by recruitment strategies in Mexico and other countries by American companies looking for workers to fill low-paying positions that most Americans will not take.[9] As a result, immigrant parents often worry about how they will pay for college even if their children have outstanding grades. Filling the gaps that exist between immigrant youths' promise and their realization of it thus requires that American employers pay their parents more than simply enough to sustain a basic standard of living.

Third, all immigrant students who wish to do so would have the opportunity to attend college. Related to some immigrant parents' financial worries about sending their children to college are concerns about financial aid eligibility if they are undocumented. Questions about documentation status were not part of my interview protocol, so I have no way of knowing the extent to which, if at all, this issue affects the particular group of students profiled in this book. What is clear from the work of other researchers such as William Pérez, however, is that many high-achieving immigrant students who are undocumented face considerable barriers trying to enter, pay for, and complete college and to work in the United States once they have graduated.[10] As current U.S. law stands, students born outside the country are not eligible for federal financial aid if they are undocumented, even if they immigrated as young children, have lived the vast majority of their lives in the United States, and have little or no memory of life in their countries of origin. As this book went to press, only thirteen of the fifty states allowed undocumented students to receive in-state tuition at their state colleges and universities, and in just three states (California, New Mexico, and Texas) were students eligible for state-level financial aid.[11]

In addition to the financial challenge of college attendance, immigrant students who are undocumented must also attend college under a cloud of worry that even if they graduate and excel, they will not be able to work in the United States because they are not eligible for a Social Security number or any residency status that allows them to hold a job. As Pérez's research has suggested, even the most promising students may stop trying if they realize they will not have the opportunity to apply what they have learned in a profession of their choice.[12] A national remedy to these conditions was proposed in Congress in 2001. The Development, Relief, and Education of Alien Minors (DREAM) Act would allow undocumented high school (or GED) graduates to apply for conditional status, which would in essence grant them six years of legal residence in which to attend college, serve in the U.S. military, or both. At the end of the six-year period, students who graduate from college and/or serve at least two years in the military could then be granted permanent-residency status, which would allow them to work in the United States. Despite more than a decade of debate, the DREAM Act has yet to pass.[13] In June 2012 President Barack Obama issued an executive order making young undocumented immigrants who are high school graduates, GED recipients, or honorably discharged military personnel eligible to apply for temporary deferral from deportation and for work permits.[14] This new law certainly represents a step forward in that it allows undocumented immigrant students to attend college and work without doing so under the constant threat of deportation. It offers no path to citizenship, however, and does not address the issue of access to in-state college tuition or financial aid. Thus, considerably more change is still needed to ensure that these young people can pay for college and achieve a level of legal status such that they are able to realize fully their ambitions to make valuable contributions to society.

Fourth, immigrant youth would be viewed as assets, not threats, to U.S. society. Although it may sound extreme to suggest that people would actually view children and teenagers as a threat to the American way of life, much of the current rhetoric about the people who immigrate here suggests otherwise. Many of our current policy debates about immigration are based on fears—fear that the English language is in danger, fear that immigrants are taking jobs away from native-born American citizens, fear that immigrants are changing the United States in a way it has never been changed before—all fears for which there is strong evidence to the contrary.[15] Portes and Rumbaut capture these fears, and the insidious racism associated with them, in their description of this phenomenon. They also point out how attitudes about immigration in the U.S. are often based on the misconception that immigrants are invading the United States in great numbers completely on their own, with no recognition of the complex social and economic relationships between the United States and other countries that are involved:

> The general perception of the foreign population among the native-born is not grounded in an understanding of the historical linkages between the United States and the countries of origin or by knowledge of the economic and social forces driving the phenomenon. The public view is guided instead by surface impressions. When foreign accents and faces are new, they are ignored. However, when they grow in number and concentrate in visible spaces, they trigger increasing apprehension. Natives are put on the defensive, fearing that their way of life and their control of the levers of political and economic power will be lost to the newcomers. The sentiment is expressed in familiar outcries such as "the end of white

*America," the "mongrelization of the race," "the rise of 'Mexifornia,'"
and "the Hispanic challenge."*[16]

One perception is accurate: the United States is changing, just as it
has changed continuously through waves of immigration going all the
way back to its founding. The current generation of immigrant students
is in many ways the future of the United States: children from immigrant families will make up nearly a third of all children in American
society by the year 2040.[17] The young people profiled in this book represent some of the best and brightest of this cohort. If we rise to the
challenge of nurturing their full potential, it will not be something we
do out of charity for the "huddled masses" we have magnanimously allowed to enter our borders. Rather, it will be out of recognition of the
tremendous assets they possess not only for their own growth but for our
society's. The voices heard here are not those of youth who wish to con-
sume the goods of America and give nothing back. They are bright, caring young people who are working hard toward getting their chance to
make the United States and the world a better place. Given their bound-
less potential, they are our best hope for a future filled with promise.

Interviewer's Note

WHEN I BEGAN conducting the interviews for *Portraits of Promise*, I admit that I did not think much about myself. As a scholar of adolescent development, the editor of two editions of *Adolescents at School*, and a former high school teacher, I have long been interested in how young people negotiate this stage of life in which physical changes, peer pressure and social networks, family expectations, academic and career goals, and other forces converge. In addition, I have had a particular interest in how young people from socially marginalized groups develop a positive sense of self amid cultural racism, sexism, homophobia, and other factors that might lead them to question their own capabilities. In this context, the challenges facing youth who immigrate to the United States—and must figure out what it means to be a teenager in a culture and language different from the one to which they were born—have seemed especially daunting to me. I have marveled at immigrant adolescents who succeed under what seem to this U.S.-born writer to be overwhelmingly difficult circumstances, so I was interested in finding out more about how and why. Yet I began by approaching these questions at a distance. It has only been upon further reflection about the stories participants told me that I have begun to consider them alongside my own.

Like the students profiled in *Portraits of Promise*, I had good grades in middle and high school and would probably have been characterized by my teachers as a "successful" student. Neither my parents nor I were immigrants, however, and I grew up speaking only English. From kindergarten through twelfth grade, I never attended school outside the United States—or even outside my suburban New Jersey school district—so I never had to adjust to a new set of cultural, linguistic, or scholastic expectations in the ways that many of the interview participants did. In addition, as a white student, I never had to deal with the racism that some of the *Portraits* students said they encountered from peers and even teachers.

My grandparents on both sides immigrated to the United States from Eastern Europe in the early part of the twentieth century, and although only one of them lived long enough for me to know her (my maternal grandmother), they seem to have instilled in my parents the classic immigrant desire for upward social mobility. Neither of my parents had the opportunity to attend college, so like many of the parents of the *Portraits of Promise* students, they had high hopes that their children would do so and thus raise our family to the next level socially and economically in the third U.S. generation. My eldest brother carried this ambition all the way to a doctorate at MIT, and as the seventh of eight children, I benefited from a family culture in which higher education was already an established value and expectation (problematically, though, primarily for males). I also benefited from the knowledge that my older siblings had accrued about the college application, financial aid, and standardized testing processes such that when it was my turn, I had a clear plan, and my ability to move on to college was never in question. Having graduated from college in the 1980s, I paid for my education in a much more generous financial aid environment than the one that exists today. Although our family could never have afforded the full tuition of the private university I chose (Northwestern), financial aid packages were generous in those days, tuition was a fraction of what it is now, and I graduated with a level of debt that would be the envy of many college undergraduates today.

As I did, the students profiled in this book seem to have strong bases of support among their families, teachers, and peers. But I worry about all the promising immigrant students without such support, and about how many times in the interviews I heard the refrain, "My family doesn't have much money." In considering both my connections to the participants' experiences and the privileges I have had to achieve my academic goals, I am all the more convinced that deliberate efforts to change school practices, government policies, and societal values are necessary to ensure that promising immigrant students get all the chances they deserve.

NOTES

Foreword

1. Ruiz-de-Velasco, Jorge, Michael Fix, and Beatriz Chu Clewell. *Overlooked and Underserved: Immigrant Students in U.S. Secondary Schools*. Washington, D.C.: Urban Institute, 2000; Suárez-Orozco, Carola, Marcelo M. Suárez-Orozco, and Irina Todorova. *Learning a New Land: Immigrant Students in American Society*. Cambridge, MA: Belknap Press of Harvard University Press, 2008.
2. Ruiz-de-Velasco, Fix, and Clewell, *Overlooked and Underserved*.

Introduction

1. Hernandez, Donald J. "Children of Immigrants: Health, Adjustment, and Public Assistance." In *Children of Immigrants: Health, Adjustment, and Public Assistance*, 1–18. Washington, DC: National Academy Press, 1999; Portes, Alejandro, and Rubén G. Rumbaut. *Immigrant America: A Portrait*. 3rd ed. Berkeley: University of California Press, 2006; Sadowski, Michael. "Teaching the New Generation of U.S. Students." Introduction to *Teaching Immigrant and Second-language Students: Strategies for Success*, 1–6. Harvard Education Letter Spotlight Series 2. Cambridge, MA: Harvard Education Press, 2004; Suárez-Orozco, Carola, Marcelo M. Suárez-Orozco, and Irina Todorova. *Learning a New Land: Immigrant Students in American Society*. Cambridge, MA: Belknap Press of Harvard University Press, 2008.
2. Portes and Rumbaut, *Immigrant America*; Stanton-Salazar, Ricardo D. *Manufacturing Hope and Despair: The School and Kin Support Networks of U.S.-Mexican Youth*. Sociology of Education Series. New York: Teachers College Press, 2001.
3. Kao, Grace. "Psychological Well-Being and Educational Achievement Among Immigrant Youth." In *Children of Immigrants: Health, Adjustment, and Public Assistance*, edited by Donald J. Hernandez, 410–77. Washington, DC: National Academy Press, 1999; Menjívar, Cecilia. "Long-term Family Separations and Unaccompanied Children's Lives: A Response to

Aryah Somers." *International Migration* 49, no. 5 (October 2011): 17–19; Pérez, William. *Americans by Heart: Undocumented Latino Students and the Promise of Higher Education.* Multicultural Education Series. New York: Teachers College Press, 2012; Suárez-Orozco, Suárez-Orozco, and Todorova, *Learning a New Land;* Sutner, Shaun. "How Schools Can Help Refugee Students." In *Teaching Immigrant and Second-language Students: Strategies for Success*, edited by Michael Sadowski, 69–76. Harvard Education Letter Spotlight Series 2. Cambridge, MA: Harvard Education Press, 2004.

4. Valenzuela, Angela. *Subtractive Schooling: U.S.-Mexican Youth and the Politics of Caring.* Albany, NY: State University of New York Press, 1999.
5. Portes and Rumbaut, *Immigrant America.*
6. Valenzuela, *Subtractive Schooling.*
7. In addition to the research about immigrant students, this list draws loosely on relevant aspects of Search Institute's Developmental Assets framework, which is based on an extensive review of adolescent development literature as well as original research and which outlines the supports and competencies most strongly associated with positive developmental trajectories for youth. See Peter Scales, Nancy Leffert, and Richard M. Lerner. *Developmental Assets: A Synthesis of the Scientific Research on Adolescent Development.* Minneapolis: Search Institute, 1999.
8. Suárez-Orozco, Suárez-Orozco, and Todorova, *Learning a New Land.*
9. Scales, Leffert, and Lerner, *Developmental Assets.*
10. Pedraza, Silvia. "Origins and Destinies: Immigration, Race, and Ethnicity in American History." In *Origins and Destinies: Immigration, Race, and Ethnicity in America*, edited by Silvia Pedraza and Rubén G. Rumbaut, 1–20. Belmont, CA: Wadsworth, 1996; Portes and Rumbaut, *Immigrant America.*
11. Suárez-Orozco, Suárez-Orozco, and Todorova, *Learning a New Land*, 35.
12. Suárez-Orozco, Suárez-Orozco, and Todorova, *Learning a New Land*, 42–48.
13. Sadowski, Michael. "Real Adolescents." Introduction to *Adolescents at School: Perspectives on Youth, Identity, and Education*, 1–9. 2nd ed. Cambridge, MA: Harvard Education Press, 2008.
14. The names of the schools are pseudonyms.
15. Suárez-Orozco, Suárez-Orozco, and Todorova, *Learning a New Land.*

The New York and California Students

1. The names of all students, as well as all other people and places that participants mentioned or with which they were involved, are pseudonyms.

To protect participants' anonymity further, in a few rare instances where necessary I have slightly altered minor details irrelevant to the research questions.

2. Stanton-Salazar, Ricardo D. *Manufacturing Hope and Despair: The School and Kin Support Networks of U.S.-Mexican Youth.* Sociology of Education Series. New York: Teachers College Press, 2001.

3. Gándara, Patricia C. *Over the Ivy Walls: The Educational Mobility of Low-income Chicanos.* Albany, NY: State University of New York Press, 1995; Portes, Alejandro, and Rubén G. Rumbaut. *Immigrant America: A Portrait.* 3rd ed. Berkeley: University of California Press, 2006.

4. Valenzuela, Angela. *Subtractive Schooling: U.S.-Mexican Youth and the Politics of Caring.* Albany, NY: State University of New York Press, 1999.

5. Tatum, Beverly Daniel. *"Why Are All the Black Kids Sitting Together in the Cafeteria?" and Other Conversations About Race.* Rev. ed. New York: Basic Books, 1997.

6. Suárez-Orozco, Carola, Marcelo M. Suárez-Orozco, and Irina Todorova. *Learning a New Land: Immigrant Students in American Society.* Cambridge, MA: Belknap Press of Harvard University Press, 2008.

7. Stanton-Salazar, *Manufacturing Hope and Despair.*

8. Raleigh, Elizabeth, and Grace Kao. "Do Immigrant Minority Parents Have More Consistent College Aspirations for Their Children?" *Social Science Quarterly* 91, no. 4 (December 2010): 1083–1102; Auerbach, Susan. "'If the Student Is Good, Let Him Fly': Moral Support for College among Latino Immigrant Parents." *Journal of Latinos and Education* 5, no. 4 (October 2006): 275–92; Mines, Richard. "Children in Immigrant and Nonimmigrant Farmworker Families: Findings from the National Agricultural Workers Survey." In *Children of Immigrants: Health, Adjustment, and Public Assistance,* edited by Donald J. Hernandez, 620–58. Washington, DC: National Academy Press, 1999; Stanton-Salazar, *Manufacturing Hope and Despair.*

9. Bronfenbrenner, Urie. *The Ecology of Human Development: Experiments by Nature and Design.* Cambridge, MA: Harvard University Press, 1979.

The Portraits

Omar

1. In order to provide a greater sense of immediacy, I use the present tense to describe conversations that took place in the one-on-one interviews.

2. Kao, Grace. "Psychological Well-Being and Educational Achievement Among Immigrant Youth." In *Children of Immigrants: Health, Adjustment, and Public Assistance*, edited by Donald J. Hernandez, 410–77. Washington, DC: National Academy Press, 1999; Suárez-Orozco, Carola, Marcelo M. Suárez-Orozco, and Irina Todorova. *Learning a New Land: Immigrant Students in American Society.* Cambridge, MA: Belknap Press of Harvard University Press, 2008.
3. Stanton-Salazar, Ricardo D. *Manufacturing Hope and Despair: The School and Kin Support Networks of U.S.-Mexican Youth.* Sociology of Education Series. New York: Teachers College Press, 2001.
4. Suárez-Orozco, Suárez-Orozco, and Todorova, *Learning a New Land.*
5. Erikson, Erik H. *Identity: Youth and Crisis.* New York: W.W. Norton, 1968; Nakkula, Michael. "Identity and Possibility: Adolescent Development and the Potential of Schools." In *Adolescents at School: Perspectives on Youth, Identity, and Education*, edited by Michael Sadowski, 11–21. 2nd ed. Cambridge, MA: Harvard Education Press, 2008; Rhodes, Jean E. *Stand by Me: The Risks and Rewards of Mentoring Today's Youth.* Cambridge, MA.: Harvard University Press, 2002.
6. Kao, "Psychological Well-Being."
7. Lucas, Tamara. "Language, Schooling, and the Preparation of Teachers for Linguistic Diversity." In *Teacher Preparation for Linguistically Diverse Classrooms: A Resource for Teacher Educators*, 3–17. New York: Routledge, 2011; Lucas, Tamara, and Ana Maria Villegas. "A Framework for Preparing Linguistically Responsive Teachers." In *Teacher Preparation for Linguistically Diverse Classrooms: A Resource for Teacher Educators*, edited by Tamara Lucas, 55–72. New York: Routledge, 2011.
8. Portes, Alejandro, and Rubén G. Rumbaut. *Immigrant America: A Portrait.* 3rd ed. Berkeley: University of California Press, 2006.
9. Portes and Rumbaut, *Immigrant America;* Stanton-Salazar, *Manufacturing Hope and Despair;* Suárez-Orozco, Suárez-Orozco, and Todorova, *Learning a New Land.*

Diana
1. Valenzuela, Angela. "'Desde entonces, soy Chicana': A Mexican Immigrant Student Resists Subtractive Schooling." In *Adolescents at School: Perspectives on Youth, Identity, and Education*, edited by Michael Sadowski, 70–74. 2nd ed. Cambridge, MA: Harvard Education Press, 2008.

2. Kao, Grace. "Psychological Well-Being and Educational Achievement Among Immigrant Youth." In *Children of Immigrants: Health, Adjustment, and Public Assistance,* edited by Donald J. Hernandez, 410–77. Washington, DC: National Academy Press, 1999; Suárez-Orozco, Carola, Marcelo M. Suárez-Orozco, and Irina Todorova. *Learning a New Land: Immigrant Students in American Society.* Cambridge, MA: Belknap Press of Harvard University Press, 2008.

3. Stefanakis, Evangeline Harris. "Assessing Young Immigrant Students." In *Teaching Immigrant and Second-language Students: Strategies for Success,* edited by Michael Sadowski, 21–31. Harvard Education Letter Spotlight Series 2. Cambridge, MA: Harvard Education Press, 2004.

4. Ward, Janie Victoria. "Uncovering Truths, Recovering Lives: Lessons of Resistance in the Socialization of Black Girls." In *Urban Girls Revisited: Building Strengths,* edited by Bonnie J. Ross Leadbeater and Niobe Way, 243–60. New York: New York University Press, 2007.

5. Moore, James L., Octavia Madison-Colmore, and Dionne M. Smith. "To Prove-Them-Wrong Syndrome: Voices from Unheard African-American Males in Engineering Disciplines." *Journal of Men's Studies* 12, no. 1 (Fall 2003): 61 73.

Ricky

1. Gaytán, Francisco X. "'Don't Be Like Me': The Paradox of a Strong Ethnic Identity among Mexican American Youth in New York City." Working paper, Northeastern Illinois University, Chicago, IL, n.d.

2. Gibson, Margaret A., and Nicole D. Hidalgo. "Bridges to Success in High School for Migrant Youth." *Teacher College Record* 111, no. 3 (March 2009): 683–711; Mines, Richard. "Children in Immigrant and Nonimmigrant Farmworker Families: Findings from the National Agricultural Workers Survey." In *Children of Immigrants: Health, Adjustment, and Public Assistance,* edited by Donald J. Hernandez, 620–58. Washington, DC: National Academy Press, 1999.

3. Auerbach, Susan. "'If the Student Is Good, Let Him Fly': Moral Support for College among Latino Immigrant Parents." *Journal of Latinos and Education* 5, no. 4 (October 2006): 275–92; Raleigh, Elizabeth, and Grace Kao. "Do Immigrant Minority Parents Have More Consistent College Aspirations for Their Children?" *Social Science Quarterly* 91, no. 4 (December 2010): 1083–1102.

4. Stanton-Salazar, Ricardo D. *Manufacturing Hope and Despair: The School and Kin Support Networks of U.S.-Mexican Youth*. Sociology of Education Series. New York: Teachers College Press, 2001; Gándara, Patricia C. *Over the Ivy Walls: The Educational Mobility of Low-income Chicanos*. Albany, NY: State University of New York Press, 1995.
5. Stanton-Salazar, *Manufacturing Hope and Despair*, 105.
6. González, Norma, Luis C. Moll, and Cathy Amanti. *Funds of Knowledge: Theorizing Practice in Households, Communities, and Classrooms*. Mahwah, NJ: L. Erlbaum Associates, 2005.

Karla

1. I have used the spelling "Hondurian" to capture more accurately Karla's pronunciation of the word for people from Honduras, which in English is usually spelled "Honduran."
2. Suárez-Orozco, Carola, Marcelo M. Suárez-Orozco, and Irina Todorova. *Learning a New Land: Immigrant Students in American Society*. Cambridge, MA: Belknap Press of Harvard University Press, 2008.
3. Suárez-Orozco, Suárez-Orozco, and Todorova. *Learning a New Land*; Menjívar, Cecilia. "Long-term Family Separations and Unaccompanied Children's Lives: A Response to Aryah Somers." *International Migration* 49, no. 5 (October 2011): 17–19.
4. Menjívar, "Long-term Family Separations."

Ibrahim

1. Merriam-Webster defines *salaam alaikum* as a traditional greeting among Muslims meaning "peace to you."
2. Stanton-Salazar, Ricardo D. *Manufacturing Hope and Despair: The School and Kin Support Networks of U.S.-Mexican Youth*. Sociology of Education Series. New York: Teachers College Press, 2001; Portes, Alejandro, and Rubén G. Rumbaut. *Immigrant America: A Portrait*. 3rd ed. Berkeley: University of California Press, 2006.
3. Sirin, Selcuk R., and Michelle Fine. *Muslim American Youth: Understanding Hyphenated Identities through Multiple Methods*. New York: New York University Press, 2008.
4. Portes and Rumbaut, *Immigrant America*, 267. Portes and Rumbaut use the term "selective acculturation" in this context to refer to second-generation youth, but it can also be relevant to youth who themselves are immigrants.

5. Portes and Rumbaut, *Immigrant America*.

6. Rumbaut, Rubén G. "Origins and Destinies: Immigration, Race, and Ethnicity in Contemporary America." In *Origins and Destinies: Immigration, Race, and Ethnicity in America*, edited by Silvia Pedraza and Rubén G. Rumbaut, 21–42. Belmont, CA: Wadsworth, 1996.

7. Stanton-Salazar, *Manufacturing Hope and Despair*.

Eduardo

1. Suárez-Orozco, Carola, Desirée Baolian Qin, and Ramona Fruja Amthor. "Adolescents from Immigrant Families: Relationships and Adaptation in School." In *Adolescents at School: Perspectives on Youth, Identity, and Education*, edited by Michael Sadowski, 51–69. 2nd ed. Cambridge, MA.: Harvard Education Press, 2008. Scholars differ somewhat on the linguistic and cultural characteristics that define the 1.5 generation, but in this context this general definition seems the most useful.

2. Stanton-Salazar, Ricardo D. *Manufacturing Hope and Despair: The School and Kin Support Networks of U.S.-Mexican Youth*. Sociology of Education Series. New York: Teachers College Press, 2001, 168.

3. For a discussion of the concept of resilience as successful adaptation in spite of conditions that might predict risk, see Bonnie J. Ross Leadbeater, Introduction to *Urban Girls Revisited: Building Strengths*, edited by Bonnie J. Ross Leadbeater and Niobe Way (New York: New York University Press, 2007), 8–9.

4. For a discussion of the risks to which youth from immigrant families are vulnerable as they acculturate to American society, see Alejandro Portes and Rubén G. Rumbaut, *Immigrant America: A Portrait*, 3rd ed. (Berkeley: University of California Press, 2006), 192.

Juanita

1. Suárez-Orozco, Carola, Marcelo M. Suárez-Orozco, and Irina Todorova. *Learning a New Land: Immigrant Students in American Society*. Cambridge, MA: Belknap Press of Harvard University Press, 2008. (See, for example, "Jane" case study, 273–84.)

2. Igoa, Cristina. *The Inner World of the Immigrant Child*. New York: St. Martin's Press, 1995, 38.

3. Igoa, *Inner World*, 38.

4. Stefanakis, Evangeline Harris. "Assessing Young Immigrant Students." In *Teaching Immigrant and Second-language Students: Strategies for Success*,

edited by Michael Sadowski, 21–31. Harvard Education Letter Spotlight Series 2. Cambridge, MA: Harvard Education Press, 2004, 21.

5. Stefanakis, "Assessing Young Immigrant Students," 25.

6. Heubert, Jay Philip, and Robert Mason Hauser, eds. *High Stakes: Testing for Tracking, Promotion, and Graduation.* Washington, DC: National Academy Press, 1999; Nichols, Sharon Lynn, and David C. Berliner. *Collateral Damage: How High-stakes Testing Corrupts America's Schools.* Cambridge, MA: Harvard Education Press, 2007.

7. Espinoza, Roberta. *Pivotal Moments: How Educators Can Put All Students on the Path to College.* Cambridge, MA: Harvard Education Press, 2011.

8. Suárez-Orozco, Suárez-Orozco, and Todorova, *Learning a New Land.*

Marisol

1. In Juan's interview, he said he found his parents highly supportive of him, but he believed that their ability to act on this support was limited because they do not speak much English.

2. Weisskirch, Robert S. "Feelings about Language Brokering and Family Relations among Mexican American Early Adolescents." *Journal of Early Adolescence* 27, no. 4 (November 2007): 545–61.

3. Erikson, Erik H. *Identity: Youth and Crisis.* New York: W.W. Norton, 1968.

4. Valenzuela, Angela. *Subtractive Schooling: U.S.-Mexican Youth and the Politics of Caring.* Albany, NY: State University of New York Press, 1999.

5. Tyson, Karolyn. *Integration Interrupted: Tracking, Black Students, and Acting White after* Brown. New York: Oxford University Press, 2011.

6. Nieto, Sonia, and Patty Bode. *Affirming Diversity: The Sociopolitical Context of Multicultural Education.* 5th ed. Boston: Pearson/Allyn & Bacon, 2008; Portes, Alejandro, and Rubén G. Rumbaut. *Immigrant America: A Portrait.* 3rd ed. Berkeley: University of California Press, 2006.

7. Taylor, Jill McLean, Carmen N. Veloria, and Martina C. Verba. "Latina Girls: 'We're Like Sisters—Most Times!'" In *Urban Girls Revisited: Building Strengths,* edited by Bonnie J. Ross Leadbeater and Niobe Way, 157–74. New York: New York University Press, 2007.

8. Taylor, Veloria, and Verba, "Latina Girls."

9. Raley, Jason Duque. "'Like Family, You Know?': School and the Achievement of Peer Relations." In *School Connections: U.S. Mexican Youth, Peers, and School Achievement,* edited by Margaret A. Gibson, Patricia C. Gándara, and Jill Peterson Koyama, 150–72. New York: Teachers College Press, 2004.

Recommendations for Classroom and School Practice

1. I use the term "adolescent" to refer to participants up through age nineteen in this book. For context, the National Institutes of Health (1999) defines childhood as the period from birth through age twenty-one, since this age range "spans the period when many individuals are still within the education system and are dependent on their families."

2. Sadowski, Michael. *In a Queer Voice: Journeys of Resilience from Adolescence to Adulthood*. Philadelphia: Temple University Press, 2013.

3. Bronfenbrenner, Urie. *The Ecology of Human Development: Experiments by Nature and Design*. Cambridge, MA: Harvard University Press, 1979.

4. Nieto, Sonia, and Patty Bode. *Affirming Diversity: The Sociopolitical Context of Multicultural Education*. 5th ed. Boston: Pearson/Allyn and Bacon, 2008; Portes, Alejandro, and Rubén G. Rumbaut. *Immigrant America: A Portrait*. 3rd ed. Berkeley: University of California Press, 2006.

5. Portes and Rumbaut, *Immigrant America*, 232.

6. Nieto and Bode, *Affirming Diversity*, 248.

7. Nieto and Bode, *Affirming Diversity*, 247.

8. Portes and Rumbaut, *Immigrant America*, 267. Portes and Rumbaut use the term "selective acculturation" in this context to refer to second-generation youth, but it can also be relevant to youth who themselves are immigrants.

9. Portes and Rumbaut, *Immigrant America*, 267.

10. Nieto and Bode, *Affirming Diversity*, 428.

11. Nieto and Bode, *Affirming Diversity;* Suárez-Orozco, Carola, Marcelo M. Suárez Orozco, and Irina Todorova. *Learning a New Land: Immigrant Students in American Society*. Cambridge, MA: Belknap Press of Harvard University Press, 2008; Valdés, Guadalupe, *Con Respeto: Bridging the Distances between Culturally Diverse Families and Schools: An Ethnographic Portrait*. New York: Teachers College Press, 1996.

12. Heubert, Jay Philip, and Robert Mason Hauser, eds. *High Stakes: Testing for Tracking, Promotion, and Graduation*. Washington, DC: National Academy Press, 1999; Nichols, Sharon Lynn, and David C. Berliner. *Collateral Damage: How High-stakes Testing Corrupts America's Schools*. Cambridge, MA: Harvard Education Press, 2007.

13. Heubert and Hauser, *High Stakes*.

14. Nichols and Berliner, *Collateral Damage*.

15. Some public schools in New York City, for example, have been granted waivers for certain portions of the Regents exam and are allowed to

substitute performance-based assessments (i.e., portfolio work) in these cases.

16. Suárez-Orozco, Suárez-Orozco, and Todorova, *Learning a New Land*.

17. Stanton-Salazar, Ricardo D. *Manufacturing Hope and Despair: The School and Kin Support Networks of U.S.-Mexican Youth*. Sociology of Education Series. New York: Teachers College Press, 2001, 267.

18. For a discussion of debates in literacy research about the time span required for English-language learners to acquire academic literacy, see Suárez-Orozco, Suárez-Orozco, and Todorova, *Learning a New Land*, 389.

19. Erikson, Erik H. *Identity: Youth and Crisis*. New York: W.W. Norton, 1968.

20. Sadowski, Michael. "Real Adolescents." Introduction to *Adolescents at School: Perspectives on Youth, Identity, and Education*, 1–9. 2nd ed. Cambridge, MA: Harvard Education Press, 2008.

21. Suárez-Orozco, Carola, and Desirée Baolian Qin-Hilliard. "Immigrant Boys' Experiences in U.S. Schools." In *Adolescent Boys: Exploring Diverse Cultures of Boyhood*, edited by Niobe Way and Judy Y. Chu, 295–316. New York: New York University Press, 2004.

22. Leadbeater, Bonnie J. Ross. Introduction to *Urban Girls Revisited: Building Strengths*, edited by Bonnie J. Ross Leadbeater and Niobe Way, 1–15. New York: New York University Press, 2007.

23. Rhodes, Jean E., Anita A. Davis, Leslie R. Prescott, and Renee Spencer. "Caring Connections: Mentoring Relationships in the Lives of Urban Girls." In *Urban Girls Revisited: Building Strengths*, edited by Bonnie J. Ross Leadbeater and Niobe Way, 142–56. New York: New York University Press, 2007, 147.

24. Rhodes et al., "Caring Connections," 147.

25. Rhodes et al., "Caring Connections," 147.

26. Espinoza, Roberta. *Pivotal Moments: How Educators Can Put All Students on the Path to College*. Cambridge, MA: Harvard Education Press, 2011.

27. Taylor, Jill McLean, Carol Gilligan, and Amy M. Sullivan. *Between Voice and Silence: Women and Girls, Race and Relationship*. Cambridge, MA: Harvard University Press, 1995.

28. Ward, Janie Victoria. "Uncovering Truths, Recovering Lives: Lessons of Resistance in the Socialization of Black Girls." In *Urban Girls Revisited: Building Strengths*, edited by Bonnie J. Ross Leadbeater and Niobe Way, 243–60. New York: New York University Press, 2007; Pitt, Alice. "Reading Resistance Analytically: On Making the Self in Women's Studies." In

Dangerous Territories: Struggles for Difference and Equality in Education, edited by Leslie G. Roman and Linda Eyre, 127–42. New York: Routledge, 1997.

29. Valenzuela, Angela. "'Desde entonces, soy Chicana': A Mexican Immigrant Student Resists Subtractive Schooling." In *Adolescents at School: Perspectives on Youth, Identity, and Education*, edited by Michael Sadowski, 70–74. 2nd ed. Cambridge, MA: Harvard Education Press, 2008; Fine, Michelle, Reva Jaffe-Walter, Pedro Pedraza, Valerie Futch, and Brett Stoudt. "Swimming: On Oxygen, Resistance, and Possibility for Immigrant Youth under Siege." *Anthropology and Education Quarterly* 38, no. 1 (March 2007): 76–96.

30. Fine et al., "Swimming"; Pastor, Jennifer, Jennifer McCormick, and Michelle Fine. "Makin' Homes: An Urban Girl Thing." In *Urban Girls Revisited: Building Strengths*, edited by Bonnie J. Ross Leadbeater and Niobe Way, 75–96. New York: New York University Press, 2007.

31. Fine et al., "Swimming"; Pastor, McCormick, and Fine, "Makin' Homes"; Torre, María Elena, Michelle Fine, Natasha Alexander, and Emily Genao. "'Don't Die with Your Work Balled Up in Your Fists': Contesting Social Injustice Through Participatory Research." In *Urban Girls Revisited: Building Strengths*, edited by Bonnie J. Ross Leadbeater and Niobe Way, 221–42. New York: New York University Press, 2007.

32. Conchas, Gilberto Q. *The Color of Success: Race and High-achieving Urban Youth*. New York: Teachers College Press, 2006; Raley, Jason Duque. "'Like Family, You Know?': School and the Achievement of Peer Relations." In *School Connections: U.S. Mexican Youth, Peers, and School Achievement*, edited by Margaret A. Gibson, Patricia C. Gándara, and Jill Peterson Koyama, 150–72. New York: Teachers College Press, 2004; Suárez-Orozco, Suárez-Orozco, and Todorova, *Learning a New Land*.

33. Rhodes et al., "Caring Connections"; Conchas, *The Color of Success*.

34. Erikson, *Identity*, 156.

35. Nakkula, Michael, "Identity and Possibility."

36. Markus, Hazel, and Paula Nurius. "Possible Selves." *American Psychologist* 41, no. 9 (September 1986): 954–69.

37. Stanton-Salazar, *Manufacturing Hope and Despair*; Gándara, Patricia C. *Over the Ivy Walls: The Educational Mobility of Low-income Chicanos*. Albany, NY: State University of New York Press, 1995.

38. Suárez-Orozco, Suárez-Orozco, and Todorova, *Learning a New Land*; Stanton-Salazar, *Manufacturing Hope and Despair*; Valdés. *Con Respeto*.

39. Suárez-Orozco, Suárez-Orozco, and Todorova, *Learning a New Land;* Stanton-Salazar, *Manufacturing Hope and Despair;* Valdés. *Con Respeto.*
40. Lucas, Tamara. "Language, Schooling, and the Preparation of Teachers for Linguistic Diversity." In *Teacher Preparation for Linguistically Diverse Classrooms: A Resource for Teacher Educators,* 3–17. New York: Routledge, 2011.
41. Valdés, *Con Respeto,* 193–95.
42. Valdés, *Con Respeto,* 197.

A Culture of Promise?

1. Bronfenbrenner, Urie. *The Ecology of Human Development: Experiments by Nature and Design.* Cambridge, MA: Harvard University Press, 1979. Bronfenbrenner's framework discusses the ecology of human life in terms of "nested" systems such as microsystems, encompassing things with which the individual has immediate contact, and macrosystems, which involve broader cultural and societal forces.
2. For effective discussions of policy changes needed to meet the needs of immigrant youth and their families, see the concluding chapters of: Alejandro Portes and Rubén G. Rumbaut, *Immigrant America: A Portrait,* 3rd ed. (Berkeley: University of California Press, 2006); and Carola Suárez-Orozco, Marcelo M. Suárez-Orozco, and Irina Todorova, *Learning a New Land: Immigrant Students in American Society* (Cambridge, MA: Belknap Press of Harvard University Press, 2008).
3. Portes and Rumbaut, *Immigrant America;* Stanton-Salazar, Ricardo D. *Manufacturing Hope and Despair: The School and Kin Support Networks of U.S.-Mexican Youth.* Sociology of Education Series. New York: Teachers College Press, 2001; Suárez-Orozco, Suárez-Orozco, and Todorova, *Learning a New Land.*
4. Orfield, Gary, and Chungmei Lee. "Why Segregation Matters: Poverty and Educational Inequality." Cambridge, MA: The Civil Rights Project, Harvard University, 2005, 8. Available online as eric Document ED489186 at www.eric.ed.gov/pdfs/ed489186.pdf.
5. Portes and Rumbaut, *Immigrant America;* Stanton-Salazar, Ricardo D. *Manufacturing Hope and Despair: The School and Kin Support Networks of U.S.-Mexican Youth.* Sociology of Education Series. New York: Teachers College Press, 2001; Suárez-Orozco, Suárez-Orozco, and Todorova, *Learning a New Land.*

6. Suárez-Orozco, Carola, and Desirée Baolian Qin-Hilliard. "Immigrant Boys' Experiences in U.S. Schools." In *Adolescent Boys: Exploring Diverse Cultures of Boyhood*, edited by Niobe Way and Judy Y. Chu, 295–316. New York: New York University Press, 2004.

7. Suárez-Orozco, Suárez-Orozco, and Todorova, *Learning a New Land;* Valenzuela, Angela. *Subtractive Schooling: U.S.-Mexican Youth and the Politics of Caring*. Albany, NY: State University of New York Press, 1999.

8. Portes and Rumbaut, *Immigrant America*.

9. Portes and Rumbaut, *Immigrant America*.

10. Pérez, William. *Americans by Heart: Undocumented Latino Students and the Promise of Higher Education*. Multicultural Education Series. New York: Teachers College Press, 2012.

11. According to data from the National Conference of State Legislatures (NCSL) and the College Board, states in which undocumented students who meet certain requirements are eligible for in-state tuition are California, Connecticut, Illinois, Kansas, Maryland, Nebraska, New Mexico, New York, Oklahoma, Rhode Island, Texas, Utah, and Washington. Wisconsin enacted a law in 2009 but then revoked it in 2011. According to the NCSL: "The states that have passed laws to allow undocumented students to receive in-state tuition delineate requirements for eligibility. In general, students must live in state and attend high school for a specified period (1–4 years), and graduate or receive their GED. Students must be accepted to a public college or university, and must sign an affidavit stating their intention to file for legal immigration status." See the NCSL website "Undocumented Student Tuition: State Action" at www .ncsl.org/issues-research/educ/undocumented-student-tuition-state-action. aspx. See also Rincón, Alejandra. "Repository of Resources for Undocumented Students." New York: The College Board, 2012. http://professionals .collegeboard.com/profdownload/Repository-Resources-Undocumented-Students_2012.pdf.

12. Pérez, *Americans by Heart*.

13. Young people eligible for college completion under the Dream Act would be those who enter the U.S. before age sixteen, have lived continuously in the United States for five years prior to the bill's enactment, have a high school diploma or GED, and demonstrate "good moral character."

14. The executive order applies to undocumented immigrants younger than age thirty who have lived in the United States for more than five years and

immigrated to the U.S. before age sixteen. The deferrals are for two years, after which individuals may reapply.

15. Pedraza, Silvia. "Origins and Destinies: Immigration, Race, and Ethnicity in American History." In *Origins and Destinies: Immigration, Race, and Ethnicity in America*, edited by Silvia Pedraza and Rubén G. Rumbaut, 1–20. Belmont, CA: Wadsworth, 1996; Portes and Rumbaut, *Immigrant America*.
16. Portes and Rumbaut, *Immigrant America*, 346.
17. Suárez-Orozco, Suárez-Orozco, and Todorova, *Learning a New Land*.

ACKNOWLEDGMENTS

First and most important, this book obviously never would have been possible without the generous and thoughtful contributions of the participants and their willingness to tell their stories. I truly believe the generosity these young people demonstrated in our interviews will help make schools better places for the immigrant students who come after them. I dedicate this book to all the *Portraits of Promise* youth and believe they should feel very proud of the contributions they have made to this project, especially for helping teachers, school administrators, parents, policymakers, and others understand better the factors that help immigrant students succeed.

In addition to the students, many faculty, administrators, counselors, and staff at CCS and NYGHS generously gave of their time, knowledge, and expertise. The interviews would not have been possible without their efforts and coordination, and their assistance in helping me gain access to transcripts, schedules, student work, and other materials—as well as their help in reserving space to conduct the interviews—proved invaluable to the entire project. The community coordinator at NYGHS played an especially active and constant role in this regard, helping me organize class visits, design recruitment materials, coordinate the focus groups, and much more. The interviews there simply would not have been possible without her. My only regret is that, because of the need to protect the anonymity of the participants, I am unable to mention any of these generous professionals by name. They are truly heroes for the outstanding work they do with these and other students every day.

The idea for *Portraits of Promise* began with a conversation with Caroline Chauncey, editor-in-chief of Harvard Education Press. Without

Caroline's vision and dedication—as well as her ability to gently keep me on schedule—this book likely would never have come to fruition. I will always be grateful for Caroline's belief in the value of my work on this project and others. Similarly, Douglas Clayton, director of Harvard Education Publishing Group, has been a constant and wonderful advocate and driving force behind getting my work into print—and, more important, into the hands of educators who can use it to teach their students more effectively. As publishers, both Doug and Caroline put students first in their work, and I am immensely grateful to have had the opportunity to collaborate with them on this project that is, ultimately, "about the kids."

Carola Suárez-Orozco is truly a leader in the field of research about the issues that affect immigrant youth. I am deeply grateful to Carola not only for the inspiration of her work, which captures with clarity and urgency the needs of these young people, but for her specific assistance with and advice on this project and for her sharing of the Longitudinal Immigrant Student Adaptation protocols, which formed the foundation of those used in the *Portraits of Promise* interviews. Angela Valenzuela, another person whose work has had a profound influence on the field of immigrant youth research, also provided valuable advice and counsel that helped shape this project. Serving as the discussant of a presentation about this project at the American Educational Research Association conference, Angela urged me to pay close attention to school context and to my own experience of what I was hearing in the interviews, both of which I believe come through in the portraits, thanks to her insights.

On a more personal note, I owe a huge debt of gratitude to my family and friends, who have always supported and cheered me on as a writer and who put up with me while I traveled across the country and otherwise worked to meet the various demands of this project. Most important in this regard has been the support of my husband, Robb Fessler, who not only is my strongest and most supportive advocate but who also rose heroically to the challenge of helping me organize and convert all of my citations to *Chicago* style (not an easy task for an author accustomed to APA). Given the huge amount of minutiae involved in such an undertaking, his was truly a labor of love for which I am immensely grateful.

ABOUT THE AUTHOR

MICHAEL SADOWSKI is an assistant professor in the Bard College Master of Arts in Teaching Program, based in New York City and Annandale-on-Hudson, New York, where he teaches about adolescent development. He has a special interest in issues of identity and voice among youth and is the author of *In a Queer Voice: Journeys of Resilience from Adolescence to Adulthood* (Temple University Press). He also is the editor of *Adolescents at School: Perspectives on Youth, Identity, and Education* (now in its second edition) and *Teaching Immigrant and Second-Language Students: Strategies for Success,* both with Harvard Education Press, and is editor of HEP's Youth Development and Education book series. He formerly taught high school English and theater, was an instructor at the Harvard Graduate School of Education, and was editor of the *Harvard Education Letter.*

INDEX